# Hunting and Fishing for Sport

# Hunting and Fishing for Sport:
## Commerce, Controversy, Popular Culture

## Richard Hummel

Bowling Green State University Popular Press
Bowling Green, OH 43403

Sports Series
General Editors
Douglas Noverr
Lawrence Ziewacz

Other books in the series:

*Baseball in 1889*
Daniel M. Pearson

*Cricket for Americans*
Tom Melville

For Kathy who so graciously stayed at home while I traveled to some of the most beautiful places on earth to conduct my research. We will revisit these wonderful wild places together!

# CONTENTS

# PREFACE

This book explores an area of sport sociology previously neglected by the discipline. I hope to stimulate further work in this area by examining various facets of some very controversial human activities. "Blood sports" are those events constructed by humans for sporting purposes which result in harm or death to specified animals. The major theses argued in this collection are: the blood sports manifest severe value conflicts between practitioners and opponents; humans are endlessly creative in devising contests of skill and endurance which entertain and also may be productive leisure; practitioners have elaborate rationales for their sports; these activities have and continue to experience ever increasing levels of commodification. These themes serve as a "hub" and the various chapters are "spokes" in which the author as spokesman leads the reader in a variety of directions to demonstrate the potential for further explorations of these topics.

The chapters also report my attempts to penetrate to the interior of these activities, to experience them through the eyes and emotions of the most ardent participants, that is, to provide an interior vantage point. A sabbatical leave from my academic duties was spent participating in various contemporary (commodified) forms of sport hunting/fishing available to those with the time and money. I participated in both hunts for meat (utilitarian) and hunts for trophies (dominionistic). Because the hunts were often unsuccessful in terms of reaching their primary goals (meat and/-or trophies), I was able to salvage the time by mentally converting my hunts to a sojourn-in-nature experience (Kellert, "Attitudes..." and "Policy...").

In sum, the struggles of conflicting values, competing moral crusades (Becker), and the search for meanings of controversial activities are the general themes of what follows. Although it may be unnecessary to make explicit my biases, I personally approve of sport hunting and fishing as recreational activities for humans. All the while, I recognize that many humans are profoundly distressed by the retention of sport hunting/fishing in our cultural inventory. I hope this book will shed light on the broad issues of why humans have hunted other life forms, why significant minorities struggle to preserve the opportunities to hunt forever, and how the various "blood sports" have affected several media (boys' literature and popular film) in popular culture.

I contend that I have attempted to achieve objectivity regarding my subjectivity concerning these "blood sports." The reader must serve as the jury.

I would like to thank Eastern Illinois University for granting me a sabbatical leave to conduct the field research for this book. My thanks are also extended to all those who encouraged me in this project by reading and commenting on parts of the manuscript as it took form. Several colleagues made exceptional contributions to this work and my thanks are extended to them in the endnotes!

# PART 1

## BLOOD SPORTS
## AS AN AREA
## OF INVESTIGATION

I begin by examining two issues: reasons why the social sciences have neglected blood sports and a brief history of the development of the contending sides of the pro-hunting, anti-hunting controversy.

# Chapter One

# Hunting and Fishing: Sports of Millions

## INTRODUCTION

Anthropology insists that hunting provided crucial protein and served as an important stimulus activity in the early social, and perhaps, biological evolutions of humankind (B. Campbell, 278-98). Until the agricultural revolution some 10,000 years ago, hunting and gathering were the major economic activities devised by humans. Thus, close to 99 percent of our history as a life form was sustained by hunting and gathering. Various forms of hunting were continued as sports,[1] often at great effort and expense, after they were no longer the primary means of subsistence.

Americans, by the millions, display an active interest in these pastimes/sports. The 1992 Statistical Abstract of the United States (241) reports that 18.5 million Americans participated in hunting with firearms in 1990, 41.5 million Americans participated in freshwater fishing in 1990, and 12.3 million Americans participated in saltwater fishing in 1990. Hunters purchased 29.7 million hunting licenses (licenses, tags, permits, stamps) and fishers purchased 36.9 million licenses (238). Americans spent $2.3 billion on firearms and hunting equipment in 1990; $265 million on archery equipment, and $813 million dollars on fishing tackle (242). These activities are the only two "blood sports" still permitted by law to Americans, except for cock fighting in four states.

Social scientists who conduct studies of sport, recreation and leisure have bypassed these activities, with few exceptions (Bryan, "Sociology" and *Conflict*; A. Gill; Atamian; Hummel and Foster) and for no immediately apparent reasons. In this chapter, I intend to shed some light on this lack of attention.

## THE PROBLEM

The publication of the *Handbook of Social Science of Sport* (Luschen and Sage) was heralded by a reviewer (Conway) as an impressive compilation of the areas, issues and literature in sports social science. This work includes an international bibliography of 5,147 entries, covering English, French and German publications

3

up to 1979 and other languages through 1975. When we turn to the index and locate references regarding *Hunting*, we find a total of two entries in the text and four bibliographic references. There are no references at all to fishing or to any other of what are referred to as the "blood sports."

On the other hand, we find hunting and fishing (angling articles) included in various editions of a popular-audience *Encyclopedia of Sports* (Menke). Also, *sport*, in *Webster's New Collegiate Dictionary*, is defined variously as: A. a source of diversion; recreation; B. physical activity, engaged in for pleasure; C. a particular activity (such as hunting or an athletic game so engaged in). A *sportsman* is defined as a person living up to the ideals of sportsmanship (*Webster's Collegiate* 1125). *Webster's Twentieth Century Dictionary* provides a more inclusive definition of "sport" as an activity requiring more or less rigorous bodily exertion and carried on according to some traditional form or set of rules, whether outdoors (hunting) or indoors (bowling) (1759).

In sum, the social science of sport seems to exclude or diminish intentionally the status of hunting and fishing as sports of humankind. Can this pattern of omission be explained?

### SOME EXPLANATIONS

This curious absence of attention from sociologists of sport, recreation and leisure may stem from fundamental questions about whether these activities are properly included in definitions of sport.[2] Let us assay some of the dimensions of this possible controversy.

Michener extends the definitions of sport offered earlier: those activities which offer competition of skills, entertainment to bystanders, and "should enhance the health of both the individual participant and the general society" (10-12). His list of defining traits of sport may find sympathy among sports sociologists and be a partial basis for exclusion of hunting and fishing from their substantive concerns. According to some measures of the physical demands of various activities, hunting and fishing are very low in the ranks of those promoting cardiovascular fitness (72). Also, hunting and fishing are not generally considered to provide entertainment to bystanders nor overt competition between or among participants.[3]

The issue of including hunting and fishing as acceptable sports is further contended among organizations which profess to promote the interests of the environment and its wildlife. A survey of 23 such organizations was conducted by an organization vehemently in favor of hunting (Safari Club).[4] Each organization was asked to submit its official position regarding hunting. Their responses were reduced to the following five groups:

Group 1: Strongly supports hunting as healthy and environmentally sound activity. Hunting is a major reason for the organization's existence.
>Ducks Unlimited, Inc.
>Foundation for North American Wild Sheep
>National Rifle Association
>Outdoors Writers Association of America
>Safari Club International

Group 2: Endorses hunting as a useful means of preventing harm to the environment by wildlife populations. Recognizes hunting as one of many goals promoted by the organization.
>American Forestry Association
>Izaak Walton League
>International Wildlife Foundation
>Safari Club International Conservation Fund
>Wildlife Management Institute
>Wilderness Society

Group 3: Displays mixed emotions about hunting. Accepts ethical, sportsmanlike hunting. Worries about depleting wildlife populations below survival levels. Refrains from accusing sport hunting of contributing to such threats.
>American Humane Association
>Animal Welfare Institute
>National Audubon Society
>National Wildlife Federation
>The Cousteau Society

Group 4: Officially neutral on the issue of hunting. Acknowledges that membership includes both hunters and non-hunters. Defines hunting as a peripheral issue relative to their main mission.
>Animal Protection Institute of America
>Defenders of Wildlife
>Sierra Club
>World Wildlife Fund

## 6 Hunting and Fishing for Sport

Group 5: Essentially negative toward sport hunting, especially trophy hunting. Accuses hunters of hindering survival of fittest in species being pursued for trophies.
Elsa Wild Animal Fund
The Fund for Animals

The message from these data is clear: a wide variety of organizations profess concern for protecting and preserving the environment and wildlife populations now and into the future. They disagree substantially, however, as to the role hunting plays in the pursuit of these goals.

A third explanation for the absence of attention to hunting and fishing from sociologists of sport, leisure and recreation asserts that these activities, especially hunting, are privately/personally abhorred, scorned, and avoided by sociologists. Substantial evidence supports a contention that at least the "establishment" in sociology—journal editors, organization officers, etc.—is sympathetic to a an urban, liberal world view (Lipset and Ladd). Such a world view has more recently shown great support for the environmentalist movement. It is not too great an inferential leap from political to ecological sympathies, especially since the villains, politically and ecologically, tend to be identified as various manifestations of the military-industrial complex. As I have demonstrated earlier, substantial elements of the environmentalist movement accuse hunting of contributing to a degradation of the environment.

### REASONS FOR STUDYING HUNTING
### AND FISHING BY SOCIOLOGISTS[5]

1. Hunting and fishing are popular activities in virtually all areas of America, especially in rural settings. The more typical topics of interest to sociology have involved urban places. Although many sociologists are employed in or near such urban areas, many sociologists reside and profess in less populous places. The data are accessible, therefore, wherever water or "gamelife" exist.

2. The data are accessible and may be assembled by a multitude of methods: sample surveys (Kellert "Attitudes" and ""Policy"; Dargitz, "Disillusionment" and "Inter-relationships"), interviews (Gill, "Social Circle"; Dargitz), direct observation and participant observation (Gill), and content analysis of the literature of these activities (Gill; Dargitz; Hummel and Foster). Gill argues

for approaching fishing by a combination of methods and then demonstrates the utility of such "triangulation" (Denzin).

3. Students of social stratification will find that participation in hunting and fishing varies by social class. One piece of evidence suggests that males with jobs in the middle occupational prestige level are most likely to pursue these sports (Burdge).

Another earlier study (Clarke) found hunting and fishing more common among the lower occupational categories and incomes of hunters parallel those of the general population (Hendee and Potter 143). Morris adds a more speculative hypothesis: hunting is most pursued by the upper and lower classes (*Naked Ape* 155). His rationale: the human male is evolved from forebearers biologically inclined and equipped to hunt. Hunting is a basic drive which still motivates the human male. He contends that modern work has been substituted by culture for the satisfactions men formerly derived from hunting. However, only the lower classes are likely to toil in jobs which are too repetitive and predictable to satisfy. The upper classes, on the other hand, avoid work of the kinds which satisfy the middle classes and, to compensate, strenuously pursue exciting leisure—hunting and gambling (155). In short, the exact pattern, explanation and even existence of social class variation in participation rates remain to be demonstrated.

4. Attitudes about hunting and fishing are a significant product of sex role socialization (W. Shaw; Sofranko and Nolan). I have a long-term project which involves collecting titles in popular children's literature which have a hunting or fishing theme in the stories. I am interested in the way hunting and fishing have been treated over time in those books. I hypothesize that the appearance of the hunting theme especially will decline over time and increasingly manifest an ambivalent position which reflects the surrounding culture. The preliminary results of my research are found in Chapter 9 of this book.

5. Practitioners of environmental sociology (Catton and Dunlap) might explore the impact of sport hunting and fishing on the quality of the natural environment. A substantial and persistent debate rages on over this question, as was mentioned earlier and will be discussed in the next chapter.

6. The practice of the "blood sports" has a significant economic and social impact on outdoor recreational areas. Numerous regions of the U.S. significantly alter their rhythms of life during the "season"—hunting, fishing, skiing, tourists, etc. The

impact of these rhythms on the "natives" should be of interest to students of community (Farnham). These topics are part and parcel of the process of the commodification of leisure which has generated a flurry of research in recent decades (Butsch). Chapter 10 of the present work sketches the historical outlines of this process in recreational hunting and fishing.

7. The controversy over hunting is a manifestation of contending social movements and value systems (W. Shaw). We have considered how organizations committed to protecting the environment can differ on the issue of hunting. The study of social movements should find many illustrations and empirical tests of its propositions among the historical data on the anti-hunting movement and the reactive development of pro-hunting organizations to defend hunting as a traditional sport. Chapter 2 offers some introduction to this theme.

8. The social psychology of sports should explore the intra- and inter-personal meanings of hunting and fishing to their practitioners. Bryan has initiated some promising investigations into the varying degrees to which sportsmen commit their lives to their recreations and the "social world" reference groups they enter (28-32). Part III reports my personal exploration of this theme.

9. Significant amounts of deviant behavior and crime occur in the forms of poaching and the illegal trade in wildlife products. The distribution and patterns of these behaviors should interest criminologists, especially those concerned with rural crime (Bristow; Reisner).

10. Sociobiology, a recent interest in the social sciences (L. Ellis), includes a concern for the role of hunting in the evolution of the biological bases of human behavior (Wilson; Morris, *Manwatching*). The topic of sociobiology has reopened the "nature-versus-nurture" debate which sociology supposedly resolved for itself seven decades ago (Bernard). Also, the role of hunting in the evolution of humankind has become a contentious topic in the feminist forum (Fisher; Morgan). The debate here is over the relative contributions of male-hunting and female-gathering activities to the food-stuffs and cultural inventory of early families.

The possibilities are not exhausted by this brief and arbitrary listing. For the moment, however, my sociological imagination has lapsed.

## SUMMARY AND CONCLUSIONS

The study of hunting and fishing by sociology in any of its branches has been avoided. Problems with inclusions of these recreations in the category of sport seem likely to persist as long as denotations of the concept vary as they currently do. Also, reluctance on the part of the establishment of sociology to acknowledge the legitimacy of these topics by excluding their consideration on the pages of the more central publications is likely to persist because of the liberal world view which animates the "gatekeepers."[6] Perhaps the status of these topics in sociology is a datum which gives comfort to those who argue that sociology cannot be value-free in its choice of research topics regardless of their potential yield.

On the other hand, if the profession heeds the admonition of a past American Sociological Association president (Rossi), it will become more tolerant of the applied research which has been completed on these topics. If so, more sociologists might venture to invest some of their professional energies in pursuing research commissioned by recreation management interests who can apply the results.

**Chapter Two**    **Battles Over the Legitimacy of "Blood Sports": Moral Crusades Aplenty**

## A BRIEF HISTORY OF HUMANS AS HUNTERS

Humankind evolved physically, emotionally and socially as hunters of other life forms as a source of sustenance. Morris argues persuasively that the human body is "hard-wired" to perform the activities of chasing, running, jumping, throwing, aiming and prey-killing in pursuit of its daily bread (*Manwatching* 308). The human psyche responds emotionally to these activities with excitement, adrenaline surges and heightened perception. Because humans evolved as group hunters, the evolved emotional package selected for in terms of reproductive advantage involved the capacity for cooperative pursuits of prey and emotional gratification when the group succeeded in prey-killing regardless of whether the fatal act was singular or plural. Morris suggests that the continuing human fascination with hunting animals for sport and the many games invented to offer a stand-in for actual prey-killing are all the product of human evolution (305). As participants or even as spectators, therefore, humans relive the thrills of the hunt, its risks of danger, the challenges to outwit the prey, and the final kill of the prey or its ultimate escape. We cannot prevent ourselves from reacting emotionally to the activities which lead to prey-killing however the kill is symbolized: a basket, a touchdown, a homerun, an ace in tennis, a goal in hockey, soccer, rugby, polo, a hole-in-one in golf, a bull's-eye in archery, a strike in bowling, etc.

After humankind abandoned hunting for wild foods as the primary economy because of population pressures on wild game habitats, climate changes, or other reasons, the hunting of exciting prey was preserved as a privilege by the political elites of most societies. Great efforts were expended to protect habitat to sustain populations of wild prey, to exclude the mass majority from access to these areas, to prevent the masses for even possessing any weapons which might be used in poaching the elites' wild game, or to create game parks/preserves where fenced areas concentrated wild or captured game animals so that

**10**

the elites would have reliable access to the opportunities to peruse them. Elites justified their privileged access to big-game hunting by claiming that hunting activities gave practice to the warrior class in the use of weapons, physical exertion and mental cunning, all essential skills in battle.

In any European society with significant population concentrations, hunting rights have remained attached to social status and property ownership to the present day. Landowners were/are entitled to control hunter access to the animals living on their lands and the animals were considered to belong to the land and therefore the landowner. This assumption is continued today in European legal codes and has only been challenged temporarily during times of revolution. Today hunting privileges are for sale to the highest bidder by landowners in Europe and in other areas of the world where viable populations of game (prey) species survive.

It is only fair to recognize that wild animals would surely have been reduced to extinction if they had not been reserved for the exclusive use of elites. This represents an interesting case of the unjust exclusion of majority access to a resource resulting in a socially desirable outcome: the preservation of certain animal species and their habitats.

When European colonists stepped ashore on the North American continent, they entered a wild game paradise. Early eyewitness accounts of edible wild game convince us that significant portions of colonists' larders were supplied by these species. This harvest of wild protein was not sport but economic necessity. The apparent unending abundance of wild game stocks led the early colonists to avoid recapitulating the European regulatory structure regarding access to game. Because the game stocks were so plentiful and perhaps because the colonists tended to spring from the socioeconomic levels which had been denied access to wild game at home, the game was essentially defined as a public resource like the air, woods and waters of the new lands. Take what you need and use it as you will, because there is no danger of exhausting the supplies.

The North American colonists also were strongly influenced by the Protestant/Puritan/Calvinist moral code which admonished all good citizens to work hard as an expression of faith in God's benevolence. The aim of the hard work was to tame the wilderness, bring it under the plow, thus obeying the Biblical admonition to "exercise dominion over the earth and over all of its living things." Hunting for food was productive work. Hunting for leisure or sport was a sinful waste of time. Early citizens who supported themselves and their families by only hunting were seen as skating across the shared responsibilities of all good citizens to cultivate the earth rather than to just harvest its natural bounty with minimal effort.

The attitude that hunting for wild game should be productive leisure survives to the present generation. Kellert's research regarding public attitudes about hunting found in a national sample that 85 percent of respondents approved of hunting for meat (productive leisure), 65 percent approved for hunting for both meat and recreation, and roughly 19 percent approved of hunting for trophies ("Perceptions").

The game stocks of the United States remained without serious dispute abundant and a common resource until the middle of the last century. However, the development of the railroad connecting more and less populated areas of the country facilitated the intensification of market hunting as an occupation. Prior to the railroad, market hunting had little impact on game stocks because the difficulties of transporting game before it spoiled made market hunting a local enterprise. The more populous localities which would have absorbed significant amounts of wild game were too far away from the wild habitats where the game thrived.

In contrast, the railroad made possible the rapid shipment to urban game markets of wild meat harvested just beyond, even far beyond, the boundaries of civilization. Wildfowl, upland game birds, venison, elk, antelope, etc. were taken by the millions of units and marketed in big cities back East.

## THE FIRST MORAL CRUSADE:
## END MARKET HUNTING, LEGITIMIZE SPORT HUNTING

Beginning in the early 1870s some American sportsmen from the middle and upper socioeconomic classes, who thoroughly enjoyed and vigorously pursued hunting for sport, recreation and trophies, became alarmed about the frenzied pace with which market hunting was "mining" the game stocks. This group, which included Theodore Roosevelt and George Bird Grinnell, founder of the Audubon Society, began to bombard the public and legislative halls with calls for an end to market hunting and some of the more destructive hunting methods (i.e., deer hunting with dogs in New England). The campaign to convince the public about the problem was carried on by the editorial policies of the newly created outdoor sporting magazines. Pictures of "game hogs," hunters/fishers who harvested large numbers of any game species, were published regularly. Articles about vanishing game species were also popular. The editorial efforts also included promotion of the "sportsman's code" which outlined the norms to be observed by the ethical sportsman. This included the following rules:

1. The sportsman should practice proper etiquette in the field—not crowding other hunters, not claiming more than a fair share of shooting opportunities, not taking more game than can be consumed by the sportsman.

2. Do not pursue any game species to the point of extinction.

3. Develop skill with the weapons of the hunt so that they can deliver a humane coup-de-grace to the prey species.

4. Acquire extensive knowledge of the prey species and its habitat.

5. Allow the prey a fair opportunity to escape by use of its natural defense/flight mechanisms. Meet the prey in its own environment and master it by "fair means."

6. Possess an appreciation for the sport in order to be its model representative to the non-sporting public and to pass it on to future generations.

This code was largely derived in the United States from the writings of a transported English sporting gentleman, William Herbert ("Frank Forrester") who settled in New York state in the 1830s and shared the English gentleman's sporting code in his writings about his own hunting/fishing forays. The English sporting code had evolved among the sporting elite of Great Britain, consisting of the country gentry, newly rich middle-class industrialists, and military officers and civil servants serving in foreign postings (J. Reiger).

The Industrial Revolution brought mass literacy to the English population. Many of the more literate members of the middle classes owned no property offering sporting opportunities; however, they discovered opportunities to hunt in foreign lands where they served the British Empire. Their literacy often resulted in them recording their hunting experiences and researches as amateur naturalists gathered in Africa, India, China, Canada, etc. The writings of these middle-class sporting gentlemen were eagerly devoured by the upper-middle and upper-class youth of the United States. These adventure travel books, coupled with the writings of "Frank Forrester", were cited frequently by Theodore Roosevelt, et al. as being partly responsible for their sporting interests.

The American sporting elite who were agitating for a new sporting ethic created the Boone and Crockett Club to encourage the observance of the sporting code of hunters by recognizing and publicizing prominent sportsmen who were its living exemplars.

This moral crusade had some significant impact on the conduct of hunting activities in America. Yellowstone National Park was created in 1872, largely as a game reserve for surviving American bison. In 1900 the Lacey Act was passed which outlawed most forms of market hunting. State legislatures gradually passed laws establishing hunting and fishing seasons and hired wardens to enforce the game laws. Wardens' salaries were financed largely through fines collected from game-law violators.

The rule enforcers were too few, however, and game laws were ignored by "outlaw" hunters and poachers who continue to this day to supply the demand for wild meat, trophy heads and skins, and other wildlife products (DiSilvestro).

The 20th Century began with the sporting code for hunters/fishers well established, continually reinforced on the pages of the outdoor sporting magazines, and coexisting with the much older and still surviving theme of hunting as productive leisure. The peaceful alliance between the sportsman's code and the productive leisure norm was expressed in Theodore Roosevelt's 1909 safari to East Africa in pursuit of trophies for himself, but more centrally, African wildlife specimens to be displayed by the New York Museum of Natural History. The press coverage of this safari and Roosevelt's copious writings about his adventures sparked public curiosity about the delights of big game hunting, stimulated the writing of children's books about the flora and fauna of "Roosevelt's Africa" and in general scored a home run for the sport hunting team.

The moral crusade to protect wildlife and its habitat scored other hits early in the 20th Century.[1] In 1929 the Migratory Bird Conservation Act was passed in Congress which authorized the purchase of land for waterfowl refuges. In 1934 the Migratory Bird Hunting Stamp Act was passed by Congress which required that a duck stamp be purchased by hunters and the monies used to purchase land for refuges. In 1937 the Pittman-Robertson Act was passed which collects excise taxes (11 percent) from the sale of new hunting firearms and ammunition, archery equipment, and a 10 percent tax from the sale of new handguns. The collected revenues are distributed to states on a 3-to-1 matching ratio for funding programs of "wildlife research, management and development." More recently, in 1973, the Endangered Species Act offered federal protection from hunting, trapping, or capturing any mammal, bird, or fish species officially designated as endangered or threatened with extinction.

The hunting/fishing fraternities seemed to have established the legitimacy of their sporting world-view which asserted the following:

1. Humans are naturally inclined to engage in prey-killing pursuits.

2. Prey-killing sports (hunting, fishing) offer win-win outcomes for all interests involved:

    a. Hunting/fishing are natural/traditional activities which can cement family and friendship bonds.

    b. The ethical pursuit of game is physically healthy and can be spiritually enriching.

    c. The harvest of game represents the removal of surplus stocks from a sustainable, renewable resource.

    d. The natural human desire to pursue game and the willingness to pay for that pleasure result in benefits beyond the sporting community. All citizens, as well as non-game species, benefit from the protection of game animals and their habitats. Multiple-uses of outdoor environments are cost-effective.

3. Prey-species deserve protection and respect at the species level. However, individual animals do not have rights comparable to human rights. Humans are at the top of the food chain and it is a principle of nature that no level in the chain has moral obligations to any other level.

4. In sum, the best protection for any animal species is for it to be a desirable prey-species which will insure that significant efforts will be invested to secure its survival in viable numbers in wild environments.

5. Members of the fraternity who violate the sporting code, thus threatening to incur increased levels of general public disapproval, must be effectively sanctioned.

6. Approval from the non-hunting public can be won by charitable acts exemplified by the program organized by Safari Club International to urge sportsmen to share part of their game harvests with the needy. Perhaps 150,000 pounds of game meat were donated in 1991 in this program (AP/TC, 9/25/92, CI).

7. The fishing fraternity has courted increased public approval/tolerance as well as addressing shrinking populations of fish by encouraging "catch-and-release" practices for many waters and species of fish. Barbless hooks and better holding facilities for the catch during fishing tournaments are other practices which help appease public opinion.

## THE SECOND MORAL CRUSADE:
## END SPORT HUNTING/FISHING, OBSERVE ANIMAL RIGHTS

Beginning in the mid 1970s and continuing to the present, a new world-view has been articulated which advocates the preservation of "animal rights" (Singer, *Animal...* and *Expanding...*; Regan; Fox; Bender, et al.).[2] The thrust of this world-view is that all living species are citizens of the natural world and humans have the obligation to recognize and protect the rights of other species by doing the absolute minimum of harm to them. Although this world-view takes many concrete forms, one version condemns sport hunting/fishing as the worst kind of "speciesism." Causing wild life forms to end their lives prematurely and involuntarily by human agency is equated with the Nazi death camps.

Various organizations promote this world-view: P.E.T.A. (People for the Ethical Treatment of Animals), C.A.S.H. (Committee Against Sport Hunting), Fund For Animals, and the Humane Society of the United States are major players in the moral crusade to abolish sport hunting. Totaling collectively perhaps one million members, these organizations are attempting to intrude into the recreational choices of roughly 18 million licensed American hunters and more than 30 million licensed American fishers. These "blood-sportsmen" have contributed significant amounts of money in the pursuit of their sports. The sale of duck stamps, excise taxes on sporting equipment and voluntary contributions total billions of dollars in this century. Each year hunters and fishers contribute more than $700 million to state fish and wildlife agencies. Each year most of the $14 million collected from the sale of duck stamps is used for habitat protection and law enforcement (AP/TC, 9/25/92, CI). The animal rights groups cannot pretend to approach those figures in terms of funds contributed to wildlife protection and propagation. So, what do they have to say?

1. First, they will respond that all those heralded monies spent for the "benefit" of wildlife are primarily for the preservation of opportunities for sportsmen to pursue the species with deadly intent!

2. Wildlife and conservation departments of states are protecting and managing species and their habitats for the hunters/fishers primarily since the hunters/fishers pay their salaries.

3. The overabundance of some prey-species such as whitetail deer is the result of poor management practices by the state agencies, leading to the reduction of biodiversity and the crowding of single species within their ecological niches.

4. Because overcrowded habitats are the products of human meddling, and because animals have rights, surplus populations should be relocated, given fertility control drugs, but not massacred by professional or sport hunters.

5. Appropriate tactics in pursuit of these principles involve hunter harassment at/on the "killing fields" and use of law suits to challenge the environmental impacts of hunting seasons for selected species. (The fallout from the hunter harassment tactic is that 45 states to date have passed anti-harassment laws. The other five are expected to follow suit.)

The animal rights groups are able to reinforce negative stereotypes of hunters/fishers by publicizing news accounts of the sale of illegal wildlife products which frequently include illegally taken trophies which are valued for their size by the unethical sportspersons. Mass circulation magazines contribute (unwittingly?) to this moral crusade by their occasional feature articles on the darker manifestations of the hunting urge (i.e., *Newsweek, National Geographic, Audubon*). For example, the animal rights people criticize archery hunters for the large numbers of wounded animals which are never captured. In fact, they make the point that the more skilled archers are more likely to wound at some time because they spend more time hunting and shoot more accurately than do the less skilled who are more likely to miss altogether. The animal rights warriors direct special scorn on "canned hunts" which confine the prey animals so there is no semblance of fair chase procedures. (A personal observation concerning this type of hunting will be found in a later chapter.)

Local book store chains offer titles that show children and other readers how to work for the cause of animal rights. The suggestions range from alterations of personal habits to suggestions for wording letters to newspapers about salient issues, among them ways to express negative opinions regarding sport hunting.

The anti-hunting crusade can be thought of as a modern resurgence of attempts by elites to control access to and uses of wildernesses. While past elites desired to reserve hunting and fishing rights for themselves, current elites apparently wish to end these practices for all.

# PART 2

## TECHNOLOGY
## AND FAIR PLAY
## IN THE BLOOD SPORTS

All sports are created by humans with rules which guide the pursuit of the objectives. The rules change and evolve with human progress in devising tools to assist in meeting the problems of existence. The three chapters devoted to demonstrating these assertions cover both hunting and fishing. Of course, as each chapter must point out to the reader, much more territory must be explored regarding these topics.

# CHAPTER THREE  HUNTING, TECHNOLOGY AND SPORTSMANSHIP: INTERACTIONS AND CHANGING DEFINITIONS

## INTRODUCTION

Hunting as a sport/game offers adversity, follows rules and rewards those who prevail over game with trophies, protein and other badges of mastery. The human group, not the individual, typically evolves standards of achievement which warrant rewards. It is impossible to understand fully the standards for achievement in the sport of hunting without recognition of the technological context within which the sport is exercised. This chapter explores what hunting as sport has meant to various groups in various historical times as those meanings interacted with the changing technology of the tools of the hunt.

Man's definitions of the situation as to what constitutes sport, fair chase, sporting chance, etc., and how man as sportsman observes and maintains standards of performance which utilize the latest technology while preserving appropriate levels of difficulty in the performance of the activity are what we will discover. We will find examples of technology overwhelming the standards and dissolving the activity into a diminished and less satisfying sport. Also, we will see other examples where sportsmen return to less developed tools and techniques which thus increase difficulty of performance.

## BEFORE SPORTSMANSHIP

Man has been a hunter by necessity for the vast portion of his existence as an emergent species. When environmental changes and cultural innovations melded to construct the agricultural revolution of recent millennia, man remained a hunter by choice. The retention of hunting in the cultural inventory signals its enduring appeal and rewards for those who master its techniques and rituals.

Before we enter the age of sportsmanship, however, we must travel back to an earlier age and examine what paleontologists have sifted from the earth as remains of early hunting. The record is not unequivocal. When man's forebears emerged from the forests and sought their fortune on the savannas, their physical tools were woefully inadequate in terms of strength, speed, fang or claws. Their only edge was a combination of a complex brain, binocular vision, upright posture and opposable thumbs. These traits permitted the invention of tools which extended their natural endowments. Even so, the record suggests that the earlier sources of protein were small animals, the young of species left unattended, and perhaps the savaged remains of kills of large carnivores who were driven away. The earliest tools were likely used for cutting and pounding rather than killing (B. Campbell 278-98).

The point at which humankind began the pursuit of large mammals is the subject of much speculation. Those human groups who were attracted to such protein sources were probably still very limited in their tools with which to dispatch such creatures. Therefore, such hunts probably had to be group efforts with very strict rules governing the process. The prey, often living in herds, and the inadequate technology, elicited the cultural patterns of group cooperation to drive herds over cliffs, into water, into bogs or into deep snows where their means of defense were neutralized and they could be dispatched at less risk to the hunters (B. Campbell 210-19).

Under such group conditions elaborate rules and preparatory rituals evolved. Functionally speaking, the low level of technology and the resulting uncertainty contributed to group cohesiveness. Successful hunts produced overabundant quantities of meat and sharing with those not directly involved in the hunt established reciprocal obligations for the future (B. Campbell 210).

In the ecosystems of other human groups, technology does not require group efforts. Among some South American Indians, for example, blowguns are solitary instruments of the chase and the prey are usually in dense forests or in treetops. We cannot establish when the blowgun was developed. It may be a relatively recent innovation which has superceded more crude and socially integrating technologies. The current territories of South American Indians are deceptively lush. However, they do not support dense populations and contemporary groups repeatedly divide and space themselves within the available territories (Lathrap 26; M. Harris 51-53).

## INTO THE AGE OF SPORTSMANSHIP

Hunting was preserved as a sport by the elites of groups who entered the agricultural age of recent millennia (Whisker x). Among the literate records of earliest civilizations we find mention of hunting by the leaders and heroes of the times (Blackmore xix). The youth were urged to develop and practice the skills of the chase as a means to promote health, practice of the skills of war, etc. (Hull 112, 136-38).

The hunting technology of that era consisted of metal spears, bows, swords, and nets (Hull 4-8). As the wheeled war chariot and stirrup developed as devices which exploit the attributes of the horse, these were added to the inventory of acceptable means of pursuing game. Also, hounds were bred and developed to assist man in his pursuit of his game (Hull 20-38; Brusewitz 104-09). What constituted game as well as what game could be hunted with what means were group decisions (Hull 59-105).

As the suitable beasts of the chase were reduced by hunting pressures and expansions of human populations, their pursuit became an ever more carefully guarded privilege of the ruling elites (Brusewitz 110). The records reveal the pride and satisfaction which these elites extracted from their sport (Blackmore xx).

The technology was still primitive enough to provide a great deal of uncertainty of success for the hunter and thus a sense of accomplishment when he bagged his prey. The excitement and enjoyment from the use of these tools and techniques derived from the speed of the horses/chariots, the sound of the hounds on the trail, the dangers, real or imagined of closing with the prey and imposing the ultimate mastery—death. The partisans of such doings defined the pursuit of especially dangerous species as the equivalent of acts of war (Blackmore xix).

Later, in Europe, the pursuit of the wild boar became a favorite form of the chase (Brusewitz 35). The technology consisted of spears, swords and trained hounds. However, the European boar is a durable adversary in the hunting field, tenacious of life, ferocious when cornered, although not aggressive when unmolested. The typical means of hunting involved pursuit with hounds who harried the boar until it tired or was provoked to the point of turning and ending its flight with a defensive last stand. The hunter would arrive on the scene of the fray between the boar and hounds on foot or a horse and then attempted to end the boar's life with a sword and spear (35). The spear was first used to weaken the boar. All bladed weapons kill primarily by inducing rapid hemorrhaging. When the spear was thrust into the boar, the hunter had to hold fast firmly because of the boar's durability. The boar would advance on the hunter who had speared it and actually drive the spear deeper while attempting to get at its tormenter. This often resulted in injury to the hunter.

Therefore, a sporting concession was devised. A cross-bar was attached near the spear's head which would block the deeper insertion of the spear by the efforts of the boar (Hull 134; Blackmore 7-10, 84-86). The hunter was relatively safe and his test was to retain his hold on the spear and keep the boar at bay until its vital signs had diminished to the point where the coup-de-grace could be delivered, perhaps with the shorter hunting sword which is essentially a thrusting weapon. Large swords with integral cross-pieces were used in the same way as the spear. The more adventurous hunters of the boar could attempt to maneuver near the boar while it was distracted by the hounds and dispatch it with a single thrust of the hunting hanger (sword); however, the risks of injury were substantial and generally unacceptable to the sports community. Therefore, this strategy was not recommended and not expected of the hunter who desired his performance to be judged as sportsmanlike.

The use of trained hawks (falcons) for hunting is an example of another kind of technology: humans observing animal habits and discovering the proper training methods to domesticate those animals to obey the wishes of their keepers. Other examples of this include the training of dogs, horses, ferrets, cheetahs, etc.

Hawking (falconry) is of ancient provenance (Brusewitz 40). Marco Polo witnessed their use in the Orient (Marsden 188-93) while their appearance in Europe was apparently quite a bit earlier (Brusewitz 40). As with many of the technologies we will examine, hawks were preserved for the exclusive use of elites. Within the elites, prescriptions evolved specifying what kind of hawks could be owned and used by persons of various social statuses and what kinds of game could be pursued legitimately by the various social levels (43). The thrill of hawking is visual, apparently, much as one might enjoy acrobatic routines with kites or airplanes (46). The different kinds of hawks (raptors), their rarity, appearance and visual performance given during the chase undoubtedly were the variables which determined eligibility for ownership. Also their natural prey would be important. The time and effort involved to capture, train and maintain their performance level required full-time keepers. Only the wealthiest members of the various levels of the elites could afford such recreations (49). An entirely unique vocabulary surrounded the hawking experience (50-51).

An ancient form of hunting mentioned earlier was the battue (drive) where the prey are driven by man, his assistants (peasants) or animals (hounds) to the prey's destruction by natural calamity over cliffs, into water, bogs, or merely into the range of the hunters' weapons (Brandner, *Hunting Instinct* 20-21). Such drives continue today in various sporting settings and are defined as sporting by their practitioners. Drives are conducted in various parts of the world for birds, pumas, wild boar, bear, tigers, deer, moose, raccoons, rabbits and hares. The sport derives from maintaining readiness to exploit one's opportunities if a prey appears at one's stand, post and platform. The rationales for such strategies seem to be that drives increase the probability that some action will be obtained, or that the solitary hunter cannot possibly penetrate the natural lairs of the prey. Thus, this technology increases the chances of confronting the object of the hunt and reduces the chances of injury to the hunter. The drives referred to here are those in which the hunters remain essentially stationary and the prey are driven to them, or the hunters anticipate where the fleeing prey can be intercepted in their path of flight (Gerrare 701-02). The thrill, excitement and reinforcement are produced by the sound of the tracking hounds, the anticipation of the ultimate confrontation, and perhaps, the mere participation in such a communal exercise in the mastery of nature.

Historically, some of the advanced examples of the battue were considered decadent in the judgment of some sportsmen (Blackmore xxii). In some European royal courts the hunts took place within fenced areas and the prey were released and herded past the waiting hunters who attempted to bag their victims from comfortable positions (Brusewitz 115). The only accomplishment here was in the skillful use of the weapon of dispatch. However, even here the goal was to provide the participants success no matter what the cost (Blackmore xxi). Since most definitions of sportsmanship require the prey have some chance to escape, however small, this hunting form is devoid of sportsmanship.

Hunting to the English mostly means hunting the fox from horseback (G. Reiger, "Hunting" 131). Here the central goal is not to capture, kill and eat the prey or mount its head as a symbol of mastery over some dangerous or magnificent beast. The point is for a group of humans on horseback to pursue a pack of hounds who are pursuing a fox until it either eludes them, or goes to earth. At the latter point the beast may either be dug out and dispatched or left to lead a merry chase another day. The speed and duration of the chase produce the thrills and excitement of this form of blood sport.

Fox hunting mostly replaced stag-hunting as a sport after the supply of stags diminished with the population increase in England at the end of the 18th century. Stags, however, were food for the table as well as fodder for the chase. Of course, one must doubt the quality of food provided by a stag which had been pursued to the exhaustion of its adrenal and muscular resources. In the case of the stag hunt on the continent, sometimes the stag was rescued in the end to be carted off and saved for another day's run. Most commonly, however, the huntsman approached the stag brought to bay by the hounds and dispatched it with the sword.

The technology for both fox and stag-hunting consisted of breeding horses, called "hunters", who were especially capable of jumping barriers and maintaining a brisk pace across various terrains for the duration of the chase (Self 25-27). The terrain needed for fox hunting provided challenging but not impossible barriers. Therefore, stone fences were mandated to farmers in the fox hunting areas of England. The legal system protected foxes from harm by farmers and trappers and offered some compensation to farmers whose fields were damaged by those fox hunting riders while following the hounds. Again, this was/is a sport for the wealthier elites. The wealthiest people in various areas would bear the expenses of maintaining the packs of foxhounds and all worthy (property owning) residents of the surrounding community were invited to participate in the pageantry of the fox hunt: hunt breakfasts, costumes, lunches, dances, etc.

### HUNTING WEAPONS

The following discussion does not pretend to include all hunting weapons' technologies. Space permits only the most important ones to be described.[1]

The bow and arrow, as hunting devices, originated in the dim past (Brusewitz 72-73). The effective range of the bow limits its use to close encounters of the hunting kind with smaller animals. (Some archery fanatics have insisted on hunting and killing the largest animals on earth with bows and arrows, including elephants.) The arrow is a cutting tool which kills by inducing rapid hemorrhaging of the prey. Of course, various groups have developed the arrow as a delivery vehicle for various sorts of poison; however, this technology is appropriate for subsistence and not for sporting purposes. The English developed the bow into a tool of war and the crown demanded regular practice by males (72). Some hunting was allowed to give the bowmen a more exciting target.

Today the bow remains a hunting instrument of choice by those who desire to pit their knowledge of prey habits and their own stalking and/or concealment skills against their prey. Technological advances in recent decades in the form of compound bows, which incorporate pulleys, have increased the effective range and accuracy of the instrument. Therefore, sporting standards have been modified to permit longer shots once frowned upon as too uncertain to be attempted by an ethical bow sportsman. On the other hand, some archers have recently returned to the earlier technology of the recurve or even the long bow, in order to increase the challenge of their sport.

The compound-bow innovation produced a typical reaction repeatedly accompanying each technological innovation in hunting throughout history: the fear that the particular innovation would decimate the game stocks, making obsolete accepted standards of behavior by hunters in the chase. How long ago the concept of conservation occurred to mankind is impossible to determine. History contains a repeated pattern: whenever a new technique actually causes a quantum leap forward in effectiveness, regulations governing the sporting pursuit of game are generally revised to shorten the season, reduce the bag and/or possession limits, etc..

The crossbow is an example of a device which did and continues to provoke extreme reactions among the keepers of the rules. Presently crossbows are prohibited from use as hunting tools in most hunting fields, except for use by handicapped hunters in a few states. This almost blanket prohibition may be related to the historical record of abiding abhorrence, consternation and disgust with which these devices were viewed

(Brandner, "Hunting Instinct" 42). Although the crossbow was a weapon of war, it was considered an unfair device in many quarters (Brusewitz 74-75). Crossbowmen were treated very harshly when captured. As a hunting weapon it was favored by numerous members of elites for its range, power and accuracy (75). Perhaps in war it was despised because it was rather effective against mounted, armored knights and stimulated the armor industry to thicken their plates—an early version of the arms race!

Later examples of crossbows were combined with firearms to provide multiple mechanisms for the launching of their missiles. Crossbows most typically launched arrows or bolts; however, they were also developed to fire stones or lead balls (Brusewitz 75). In the gamefields they were sporting in the sense that they were slow to reload and the user generally had but one shot. However, their low level of noise sometimes provided the opportunities for additional attempts. And reportedly, poachers greatly admired them.

The history of firearms is a complicated tale. The use of gunpowder to propel projectiles was probably first attempted in war. The early technology of guns was quite cautious, involving the construction of very heavy barrels to withstand the unmeasurable pressures of the rapid oxidation process of burning black powder. The earliest examples of guns (14th century) were too cumbersome, uncertain, and slow for use in sporting fields (Brusewitz 78). At first there was no concern that guns would decimate the sporting prey of the chase. However, as knowledge accumulated about the necessary margin of safety required to build into the containment vessels for gunpowder, the artificers began providing the upper class elites with hand-held, shoulder-braced fire arms.

The first standard form of gun for the individual was the matchlock. This device was used by pointing at the target and touching a smoldering wick to an ignition hole in the rear of the barrel which ignited the main charge of powder. This device was very uncertain, easily put out of commission by wind and wet weather (Wilkinson 14). For sporting use it was primarily fired at sitting game: ducks, geese, pheasants, quail, etc. (Brusewitz 88). In this circumstance, the powder charge propelled a quantity of projectiles which scattered upon exit and increased the chances of hitting the prey. The range was quite limited and accuracy was mediocre at best. Also, the art of compounding powder mixtures was still in its infancy and pressures probably varied because of unevenly blended components (Waterman, *Treasury* 16).

The next generally recognized technical advance was a new ignition system, the wheel lock (16th century). This was a very expensive innovation, compared with the cost of constructing matchlocks (Brusewitz 82). Instead of a wick, ignition was accomplished by a spring-driven steel wheel being rotated against a piece of pyrite held in a small clamp, mounted on an arm which could be rotated in and out of contact with the wheel (Wilkinson 16-18). This device required a high degree of metal-working skill to fabricate and thus only the richest of the elites could aspire to its ownership (Waterman, *Treasury* 16; Wilkinson 18). The wheel lock did increase the certainty with which a gun could be fired, however. Therefore, in proportion to its numbers in existence, the wheel lock was more often used in the sporting field.

The wheel lock appeared at about the same time that the rifled bore was added to the record of human folly (Wilkinson 18). The spiraling grooves cut inside the bore of a gun imparted a stabilizing spin to the projectile, thus giving it much more range and accuracy. The "rifle gun" stimulated sportsmen to devise a greater variety of uses. It became sporting to attempt to strike game animals at a greater distance with these weapons. The rifled bore did not permanently join the inventory of the means of martial mayhem until around the beginning of the 19th century. But, it made its mark on the hunting field in the hands of those who could afford its price.

Since the rifled bore afforded the means of enhanced accuracy, accuracy became a sporting criterion for hunters in many circles, rather than merely firepower: delivering the maximum number of projectiles over the largest possible area (Waterman, *Treasury* 19). Target shooting was stimulated early in the history of rifled arms. Such practice accomplished two things: preparation for both the battle field and the sporting field. Still the rifle gun was primarily used to dispatch sitting prey. (The shotgun, as its label suggests, delivers multiple projectiles toward its intended target.)

The next technical improvement among ignition devices was the flintlock (16th century) (Brusewitz 83). This device consisted of a slab of flint, held in the jaws of a small vice which was mounted on an arm, pivoting through a short arc. This arc caused the flint to scrape across the vertical steel face of an L-shaped piece of steel which also served as a cover for a small depression containing finely ground gunpowder. The sparks produced by the stroke fell into the small depression filled with powder, igniting the priming powder and thus the main powder charge connected by a small horizontal orifice in the barrel next to the depression (Waterman, *Treasury* 17; Wilkinson 19). This device was less expensive than the wheel lock, partly due to the improvements in metallurgy and metal working by the time the flintlock was developed. The flintlock was carefully made in its higher grades, and its external powder depression, the pan, had water-proof covers which made it somewhat more reliable under windy and/or wet conditions.

The French and the English refined the flintlock to an artistic piece of machinery which graced very light shotguns and relatively light rifled guns (Waterman, *Treasury* 132). The lighter weapons of the chase were also the result of the use of stronger metals which permitted thinner barrels. The reduction in weight of shotguns was exploited by the French especially who are credited with developing the physically challenging sport of shooting at flying birds while they remained relatively close to the gunner. The King of England, returning after the demise of Cromwell, is said to have imported this sporting style from France (Brandner, *Hunting and Shooting* 70-74; Trench 126). Shooting on the wing is a sporting technique which remains in high favor and has spawned many shooting games: skeet, live pigeon shoots, sporting clays, etc. (Waterman, *Treasury* 153). In fact, shooting on the wing has become the only technique to be considered sporting. Hunters who shoot sitting or even running birds, since their earth-bound flight on foot is slow, are denounced as "pot hunters", persons who are only concerned with results and not the process.

Wing shooting has evolved various sporting standards for the various species: how far away must the flying game be before it is ethical to shoot (Gerrare 704), how far is too far to insure either clean hits or total misses, thus avoiding crippling the birds, what kinds of "blinds" or hiding places and what kinds of decoys are sporting? In the early days live decoys were used to lure ducks and geese to their doom. Also bait, in the form of corn or other grains, was once permissible but no longer. Each standard seems designed to retain the element of fairness—allowing the prey some chance of escaping (Waterman, *Treasury* 132). Otherwise the sport is reduced to slaughter or mere killing.

The development of the percussion ignition system (19th century) increased the certainty of powder charge ignition and thus made hunting with firearms more possible during inclement weather (Brusewitz 87). Metallurgy also improved during the early 1800s, along with the introduction of the percussion system. These developments made possible still lighter sporting guns, both for shot and bullet. Lighter weapons enabled more sportsmen to withstand the rigors of bearing the gun afield for the time periods consumed by hunting. Lighter weapons were easier to manipulate and thus more hunters were motivated to develop the skills necessary to bag moving game.

The percussion era in Europe, 1830-70, was also the time of socioeconomic mobility for millions of persons. The expanding bourgeoisie imitated their noble, wealthy fellows by pursuing the same field sports as had been practiced by the elites since 1066 and before. Also, mass production reduced the cost of the sporting implements of the chase. And mass transportation opened access to game fields previously beyond the pale of middle class pocketbooks. Increased pressure on game populations also stimulated the beginnings of game management practices to insure a continuing supply of game stocks (as targets).

The stronger, more reliable hunting weapons in Europe were welcomed by the expanding ranks of explorers who moved about the globe, pushing back the veil of territories unknown to European interests. In Africa, Ceylon, India, Canada, the adventurers took along their hunting guns for sport in the midst of these far lands (Trench 210).

The next step in the evolution of hunting devices was the development of the self-contained metallic cartridge gun. Appearing in the latter half of the 19th century, this invention made guns even more reliable and powerful. Cartridges make possible the loading of a gun from its breech (Trench 222). This loading method is more rapid and especially aided the development of rifled guns. As mentioned earlier, the rifled barrel imparts a rotation to the projectile which induces a reliable flight pattern. The earlier technical problem was always how to insert the bullet from the muzzle end of the bore and position it in the permanently-sealed breech, over the powder charge when the bullet had to fit the grooves of the rifling. Various means were used to achieve this. One solution was to make hollow cavities in the base of the bullet which allowed an undersized bullet to be pushed down to the charge and then which expanded as the powder ignited. The expanded projectile was forced by the powder gases against the sides of the bore and, thus, into the grooves as it progressed out the barrel. Another solution was to "patch" the under-sized ball or bullet with fabric or paper. The slightly compressible patch would permit the projectile to be pushed down the barrel, onto the powder charge, but effectively sealed off the grooves when the charge ignited so that the powder gases did not escape around the accelerating projectile. Either solution produced a rapid rotation of the projectile.

With breechloading, the bullet was positioned in the cartridge case, ahead of the powder. The assembled cartridge was inserted into the breech in an expanded portion of the barrel called the chamber. The bullet was full-sized and ready to be driven through the barrel by the powder gases after ignition, needing no hollow base or patch. Heavier, longer bullets could be used and sportsmen commenced to pursue larger mammals with these more powerful calibers.

The next evolutionary step in arms technology was a significant improvement in the propellant of bullets. Black powder was limited in the propulsion pressures it could develop; therefore, the power of the cartridges was limited. Increasing the powder charges worked to a degree; however, black powder combustion produced a large percentage of solid wastes in the forms of smoke and residues inside the barrels. Larger charges just compounded the problems. The residues reduced the accuracy of rifled guns and disrupted the patterns of shot in smooth-bored guns.

Smokeless powder did much to eliminate the problems with black powder in the closing years of the 19th century, while increasing the power of the cartridges by generating greater pressures (Hinman 108). This latter trait required stronger locking devices be developed for the breechloading weapons (Waterman, *Treasury* 51). The necessary strengthening was soon accomplished, however, and the sporting use of guns continued to grow with the expanding population. Increased power of rifled guns made shooting at game at longer distances practical and sporting since the chances of successfully downing the prey were increased (116-17). However, the full acceptance in sporting circles of long range rifle shooting awaited another development to be discussed a little later.

With the advent of the self-contained gun cartridge, repeating rifles and shotguns were developed to increase the firepower of their users (Waterman, *Treasury* 53). Here we witness some disagreement concerning the sporting legitimacy of this technology. On the continent the repeating shotgun was not accepted as sporting and the double-barreled gun remained the proper arm of sportsmen (141, 156). Only in America did the repeater catch on and eventually drive the double-barreled gun off of the market. The repeater was well adapted for mass machine production while the double required much more in the way of hand operations to complete even the cheapest grades (141-44).

The first repeating rifles had relatively weak breech-locking devices and thus did not seriously compete with the powerful single-shot breechloading rifles for the sportsmen's market. This technical obstacle was soon overcome in the American arms industry as well as on the European scene. By 1900 repeating rifles were substantially every bit as strong and powerful as any of the single and double-barreled rifles on the market (Waterman, *Treasury* 118). The repeating rifle may have encouraged a decline in certain hunting skills such as stalking within a close distance to the prey. With only one shot available, the closer the hunter approached before firing, the more certain of success. At the same time he was demonstrating his skills in wood- or field-craft.

The repeating shotgun was avidly embraced by American hunters who had more abundant game to pursue than did their European counterparts (Hinman 115). However, at the turn of the century, the user of the repeating shotgun was confronted with calls from sporting magazines to exercise restraint in its use to keep from decimating the game stocks. The sporting magazines of the day began campaigns against "game hogs" and ridiculed their "accomplishments" on the editorial pages. A nascent conservation ethic seemed to emerge from among the ranks of the most avid sportsmen and their media leaders (J. Reiger 28-33). The idea gradually congealed that the hunting experience was much, much more than just the kill but instead the whole process of fair pursuit and possible but not certain ultimate capture (26). (More about this point is found in later chapters.)

During the last quarter of the 19th and early years of the 20th centuries, the Western states were heralded as the hunters' heaven. Railroad lines and others published guides as to where to go and what to hunt and, of course, offered to provide the transportation for the sportsman. The railroad opened up new gamelands and frequently was the cause of the abuse of standards of fair chase. Reportedly some gunners would blaze away at game animals as the trains passed them on the prairies. There was no means or intent to retrieve such animals. The railroads would also supply railroad cars and park them on sidings near game country so that wealthy sportsmen could enjoy hunting lodges on wheels while remaining in the areas.

Another stimulus to the development of the concept of sportsmanship was the far-flung British Empire. During the last half of the 19th century representatives of British interests, military and civilian, were spread around the world. Many were stationed for significant periods away from home and sought to replace the sport they enjoyed at home, or on the continent, with local opportunities (Haresnape viii). They sought replacement prey for those traditionally pursued. Of course, Africa offered a cornucopia of species which struck the sporting fancies of these hunters, more than ever encountered before. In India, Ceylon, China and especially in the Himalayas these sportsmen sought and found worthy trophies to collect and display at home when their tours of duty were over. Many of these hunters wrote memoirs which created interest among their readers in the places hunted.

By 1900 and following, the transportation revolution had developed to the point that many previously inaccessible places were now within reach of aspiring sportsmen. Motor vehicles, small motor boats, more and better roads made expeditions to far gamelands less expensive and therefore, more appealing to a larger group of sportsmen.

At all times during the periods we are reviewing, sportsmen employed guides of various sorts. This generic category included the professional foresters/gamekeepers of English and European gamelands who kept careful track of the individual members of prey species as they matured to the point of becoming desirable trophies. This group of professionals also culled the herds of prey so that the carrying capacity of the habitat was not strained. They also raised the fowl who were popular sporting targets, such as grouse, pheasants and quail. In other parts of the world, guides were merely local residents who, for a price, were willing to share their knowledge of local animal haunts with visiting sportsmen. Guiding was a seasonal occupation for them. Later, in some gamelands, guides became mandated by law to accompany visiting hunters to insure compliance with the game laws. The guides became the "gatekeepers" regarding sporting practices (e.g., not shooting from vehicles, establishing distances from vehicles that must precede shooting, limiting bags on various species). In the richest gamelands such as Africa and Alaska, guides became full-time specialists and the "white hunter" character emerged as a blend of fact and fiction.

On both sides of the Atlantic groups of sportsmen organized to conduct orderly competitions among trophy hunters. The goals were to establish and enforce uniform standards of measuring and judging the entries, and to maintain and publish permanent records for the sporting world. These organizations, the Boone and Crockett Club in America (Waterman, *Part* 196) and Rowland Ward's in England, had counterparts in various countries of Europe: France, Germany, various European nations, etc. (Allison 18). Periodic sportsmen's expositions were and are held in Europe to display trophies, both old and new, acquired by members of various groups.

These organizations also have always attempted to enforce sporting standards of behavior in the chase. Witnesses were/are required to submit verifications of the means by which the trophies were taken. These organizations, in recent decades, have removed certain species from their list of eligible new entries into the records (i.e., polar bears) because of either their endangered species status and/or difficulties in documenting that fair chase standards were observed in their pursuit. The polar bear, for example, has been hunted extensively from small airplanes, a practice now illegal. The pilot/guide and hunter(s) search for polar bears from the air and when a suitable one was located, the plane landed as close as possible and the hunter(s) made a final approach to the prey.

Another kind of competition exists, which is related to the variety just mentioned. The goal of collecting one of each of the varieties of the world's wild sheep species is ardently pursued by more affluent sportsmen. This quest leads the seekers around the world to the most inaccessible reaches of many continents. A more modest goal animates North American sportsmen: collecting heads of the five or six varieties of wild sheep in the Americas. The reputations of such sportsmen are darkened by association any time news surfaces about the discovery of illegal kills and sales of wild sheep trophies.

In the early years of the 20th century, various American notables traveled to distant gamelands in Africa, Alaska and India and wrote of their hunting adventures upon return. Respected figures such as Theodore Roosevelt (Waterman,

*Treasury* 104) and prominent novelist Stewart Edward White did much to glorify and validate big game hunting for the male public. Roosevelt, especially, was the most prominent American on the national scene for the first decade of this century. His participation in and description of hunting as a healthy, virile outdoor activity was shared with the public for 15 years before he became President. His early hunting adventures in the American West are still being reprinted today. He was a co-founder of the Boone and Crockett Club and pointed the way to the national government's involvement in conservation, especially the national park system. Even the anti-hunting movement has not chosen to extensively attack Roosevelt's motivations and reputation as a hunter.

Returning to more technological influences on sportsmanship, the telescopic rifle sight demands examination. This device brings the picture of the prey closer to the gunner and permits more selectivity, pre-examination of the prey, and also more accuracy in the aim of the firearm (Waterman, *Treasury* 128). For the reasons just listed, the telescopic sight is considered an aid to sportsmen. On the other hand, the improved sighting encourages hunters less skilled in stalking their prey to attempt shots at longer distances. The telescope does not aid in the steadiness with which the weapon is held; therefore, longer shots magnify the errors of holding and increase the chances of wounding rather than quickly dispatching the prey.

Ironically, the telescope can be considered a technical stimulus to the development of more powerful cartridge calibers. This was made possible by the evolution of smokeless powder and smaller diameter, metal-jacketed bullets which could be launched at higher velocities and therefore were capable of accurately striking more distant targets (122).

As the telescope sight developed and cartridge calibers were reduced in diameters, a new competition evolved: the use of the *least* powerful weapon to dispatch one's prey. The competition here was/is to demonstrate the accuracy with which one could direct a missile to strike a vulnerable spot on the animal (Waterman, *Treasury* 123). Also light (less powerful) calibers were described in some circles as re-emphasizing the need to approach the prey as closely as possible in a display of woodcraft.

At the same time, weapons' designers attempted to increase power while decreasing calibers by increasing the velocities of the projectiles. As elementary physics acknowledges, striking power of a projectile can be increased by increasing the mass of the projectile or increasing its velocity. Before smokeless powder, velocity was limited by the oxidation rates and efficiency of black powder. Increased power was achieved by increasing the weight of the projectiles. Some attempts were made to increase the calibers to the point where few humans could withstand the recoils generated. With smokeless powder, which was physically capable of generating higher velocities, greater striking forces could be generated with projectiles of the same or lesser weight. The new challenges encountered were designing projectiles which could withstand the increased rotational forces imparted to them as they were forced through the spiral grooves in the bore and follow the same trajectory time after time. Any imperfections in the projectiles in terms of weight, shape, or diameter would magnify the variations in flight paths upon exit from the barrel. As a result, the limits of accuracy and velocity with existing projectile technology were soon encountered.

With the world-wide inflation of recent years, hunting trips abroad are increasingly beyond the means of most hunters (Bradbury 67). One response to this development has been the creation of commercial game preserves in America which offer the hunter a chance to pursue exotic, imported species which have been chosen for their hunter appeal as well as their adaptability to the climate (Waterman, *Treasury* 226-30). Game, in the form of wild boars, pheasants and various hoofed prey are most common (Boddington 50-52). Controversy rages over whether the hunting experience offered is worthy of acknowledgement by keepers of sporting traditions and standards (51). Opposition seems to be easing a bit; but most sportsmen see such experiences as "pretend" and not serious hunting efforts. The commercial operators of such preserves attempt to make their services credible by enforcing some variety of fair chase standards. However, they face a dilemma: they draw patrons by records of high rates of success achieved by past hunters. On the other hand, they dare not remove too much of the chance factor because otherwise the experience diminishes in the eyes of serious hunters who demand that their prey have significant chances to elude the hunter. The preserves claim to offer various levels of difficulty to their clients in the chase. These may result from covert assessment of the hunting backgrounds of those who pay to shoot and provision of an experience which matches the best estimates of the hunter's aspirations.

Many hunting preserves only charge their clients for successful hunts. Therefore there is the economic incentive for the operator to increase the chances of success. A trophy measuring and recording organization is in existence which deals with animals taken on such preserves. The level of respectability ultimately achieved by these hunting institutions remains to be seen. (My personal experience with this form of hunting is reported in chapter 6.)

At the time of the Civil War Centennial, during the early 1960s, some adventurous entrepreneurs caused to be produced replicas of civil-war-era weapons for use with newly manufactured black powder (Waterman, *Treasury* 216). Initially, these replica arms were manufactured in Spain, Italy, Belgium, and then imported into the U.S. However, their popularity soon induced American manufacturers to get on board. In response to demand by a growing fraternity of users, various states legislated "primitive weapons" hunting seasons, especially for deer. Black powder rifles and shotguns are widely available and quite effective in practiced hands in the game fields (217). Their effective range is almost that of those modern weapons allowed in the more populated states. They are a challenge to use and keep functioning during inclement weather, offer only one or two discharges, and call upon the same stalking and concealment skills which were highly developed, according to legend, among our ancestors. More recently, within the past decade, reproductions of black powder cartridge rifles have appeared on the market and have found favor among western hunters of larger hoofed prey: elk, moose, mule deer, etc. All of these developments represent a combination of the human capacity for nostalgic, selective reconstruction of the past "golden" eras and willingness to increase the difficulty of a sport by self-imposed limitations on participants. The sense of achievement with successful use is correspondingly enhanced (Whisker 3).

Another step back from the frontier of the latest hunting technology is in the form of handgun hunting (Waterman, *Treasury* 225). Handguns are notoriously difficult to master and use effectively. Constant practice is required to maintain any level of achieved proficiency. For whatever reason, hunters seeking new challenges began use of handguns for hunting various prey. This places high demand, again, on stalking and concealment skills, and is endorsed by those concerned with hunting sportsmanship for that reason. Also, handgun makers have responded to this demand by producing models solely suited to hunting and not at all for defense, a traditional role of the handgun. These hunting models are generally heavy, of more powerful, even rifle, calibers, and capable of carrying telescopes to increase clarity and certainty in sighting (Jones 54-56). Manufacturers of such arms and accessories have promoted their use by demonstrating the handgun's capacity to dispatch the largest game on earth: elephants, rhinos and polar bears (55).

Another form of technology used in game fields is amplified phonograph records and tape cartridges. These are used in the sport known as "varmint" hunting to lure prey within shooting distance. The status of the prey: foxes, crows and coyotes are such that tricking them with such lures is less reprehensible by most sporting standards than luring deer with salt, doves and geese with grain. Many members of the varmint category are defined by humans (some) as nuisances who extract economic penalties from humans by the natural behaviors of such animals.

Technology, electronic and optical, has also assisted humans in overcoming their sensory deficits relative to animals.

> Infrared binoculars permit vision in low light. Bionic Ear, which looks like an oversize set of headphones, raises the wearer's hearing to Natty Bumppo sharpness. Trail monitors...look like the key pads of a home security system. A hunter sticks one to a tree. He leaves. For however long he's gone—two weeks, a month—the timer's infrared sensor notes the type and frequency of animals passing by. (Farnham 86)

Several hunting games have crossed the Rio Grande from Mexico and found ready acceptance in the U.S. One of interest here is silhouette shooting (Waterman, *Treasury* 177; Dunlap 193-97). The game has various forms, for rifles with and without telescopes, both high-powered and rimfire, for handguns with and without telescopes (Gates 149-50) and for black-powder cartridge rifles. The targets are animal-shaped silhouettes cut from steel plates, welded to flat bases, which are set up at various fixed ranges and fired upon by the players. The object is to knock them over. In the rifle version of the game, shooters must stand when shooting and are limited to rifles of certain maximum weights (Waterman, *Treasury* 182-84). There are several classes of pistol silhouette shooting: standing and various supported positions with standard models of handguns and extensively modified handguns in another category of competition. These games have spectator appeal because objects fall over and scores can be kept by onlookers, unlike the typical target shooting contest.

A hunting game currently experiencing dynamic growth in popularity is "sporting clays." Imported from Europe, this shotgun sport recreates hunting situations of various kinds with clay pigeons as targets. In the U.S. the available courses have increased from two in 1986 to over 200 in 1992 (Farnham 86).

A related issue in the matter of sportsmanship involves the decisions of game management departments to permit and encourage the taking of female deer by hunters. This policy has been introduced several times historically because of the carrying capacity of habitat being over-stressed. In virtually every case hunters mounted an outcry against the policy. The charge was that shooting does was unsportsmanlike (Koller 23). This is a kind of quirky, anthropomorphic, sexist position which implies that the female of the species is less able to evade the hunter. (In fact, there is some, not uncontested, evidence which suggests that as game has been hunted over the years, it has become more wary and thus a greater challenge to the hunter. Many species may have retreated to more remote wildernesses than they originally inhabited.) The superior flavor of venison from does did not counteract the opposition. Many hunters refused to take advantage of the opportunity afforded them even in the face of the argument that it was good for the deer herd and habitat.

## DISCUSSION AND CONCLUSIONS

The interplay between technology and standards of sportsmanship examined in this chapter supports the proposition that man is truly *homo ludens*. However, so far I have concentrated only on the sports community which shares the belief that hunting is an acceptable sport/recreation. This community has not ignored its public image and has taken steps to polish it. (See chapter 2.) To borrow a thought from a book on the "politics of hunting" in Britain:

> The hunting community has sought to establish a new identity for itself allying itself to modern causes. In its own eyes it has become the leading influence in conservation, its basic issue is freedom of choice, its methods involve the least possible element of cruelty, and its aims are humanitarian. The

vocabulary of its literature emphasizes the legitimate and democratic nature of its activities. (Thomas x)

However, for those who are opposed to hunting in varying degrees and for varying reasons, the evolution of technology has only made the "crime" man commits against animals more heinous.[2] To this heterogeneous group, only man pursuing animals which are capable of defending themselves would constitute "fair play." Man would have to handicap himself so that there is no edge in his favor. Even then, the anti-hunters will ask: what's the point? Why take life in the name of sport rather than as a necessity for survival and defense? If man must seek excitement in activities which permit mastery, why not pursue lifeless targets such as bowling pins, basketball hoops or soccer goal posts? Other sporting events offer the spectacle of objects falling over, being penetrated and captured. Why permit, encourage or support such atavistic customs so that they remain in modern man's cultural inventory?

To this group, the foregoing history has merely documented man's attempts to rationalize the continuing cruelty to animals in the name of sport while incorporating ever more sophisticated means of pursuing and destroying these living beings. To this group I can only say: the issues you raise are matters of value choices which were considered in chapter 2. The perspectives of those who support hunting need to be understood regardless of one's personal value stance. I hope this chapter has made a modest contribution toward that end.

# Chapter 4

A Sporting Chance:
Relationships between
Technological Change and
Concepts of Fair Play in Fishing[1]

## INTRODUCTION

This chapter examines interactions between technology and conceptions of fair play in fishing by drawing on evidence from trout and bass fishing in America. These two forms of fishing represent ideal-typical opposites and thus provide the most lucid evidence for the pattern relationships discussed in what follows.

The term *technology* refers to the tools of fishing, techniques of using these tools, knowledge about the prey and its environment, and even knowledge about the effects of the tools on the populations of prey. *Fair play* is conduct according to rules of the contest, game or sport which specify acceptable means of pursuit of particular goals. The origins of these rules may be: 1) accruals of traditions assembled in the literature of a sport (as in trout fishing); 2.) rules set by states which are enforced as part of the licensing of participants (as enforced by fish and game departments regarding techniques, hours, "bag" limits); 3) formal codes established by organizations of enthusiasts and promoters to protect the integrity of the activity and encourage formal competitions among participants (as in the fishing tournaments sponsored by Bass Anglers Sportsman Society (B.A.S.S.) and the International Game Fish Association (I.G.F.A.); 4) or personal definitions of fair play evolved by practitioners (as among certain types of trout fishers). Ultimately, compliance with these rules of fair play is internally motivated rather than externally coerced (see McIntosh 2-4; also, Fraleigh).

## THE SPORT OF FISHING

Historically, the genesis of fishing was part of a subsistence economy. Fish were caught to eat and method was irrelevant. The notion of fair play only emerged as fishing became a non-subsistence activity of the leisure classes. Ancient Egyptian and

Chinese royalty fished for recreational pleasure and sport, using angling techniques (i.e., hook, rod and line) some 3000 years ago (Rundell), while the peasantry caught fish for food by any successful means. Later, the land-owning nobility of the Renaissance reserved the better fishing streams for their personal use, excluding the masses (Gabrielson 623). Thus, sport fishing began as a leisure class recreation.[2]

Currently, the sport of fishing involves the following elements: decisions about the fish(es) to be pursued; access to their habitat; technological hardware, e.g., rods, reels, lines, bait; knowledge of the proper/effective use of the equipment; and knowledge of the habits and preferences of the fishes. All of these components constitute the technology of fishing.

Decisions about what fishes to pursue involve various considerations. Fish are attractive targets if they grow to a large size, if they are good food, if they are a rare, desired species, if they behave in predictable ways by being lured to baits (artificial or natural), or if, once hooked, they struggle to escape in spectacular fashion (Evanoff 7-12).

Knowledge of fish behavior, habitat and use of fishing equipment must be learned by fishers. This knowledge is learned by one or more of the following means: reading the sporting literature, practicing with the equipment or receiving the tutelage of a more experienced person. The capstone to the sport of fishing is the sporting ethic, fair play.

## THE SPORT IN FISHING

When fishers pursue fishing as a sport, the issue becomes, "What constitutes fair play?" Definitions vary widely by species of fish pursued, nature of the sporting event (solitary pursuit vs. tournament), and so on. Waterman suggests personal definitions of fair play in sport evolve over time; initially, the fisher wants the *most* fish as a satisfying conclusion to a day's sport (*History* 171). Later, s/he considers only the *biggest* fish as the primary goal. Finally, and more rarely, the fisher imposes on self the goal of pursuing the *most difficult* fish, either because of habitat or equipment used or situations in which the fishing is performed. Waterman's types parallel Bryan's ("Spring-Stream"; *Conflict*) typology developed from his studies of trout fishers. *Occasional* fishers, desiring to catch any fish on any available tackle, are those to whom fishing is a leisure or recreational activity. *Generalists* attempt to catch their limit using the most efficient kinds of equipment (e.g., spinning or spincasting tackle). *Technique specialists* desire to catch large fish on specialized equipment (e.g., fly-tackle). Finally, *technique-setting specialists* only attempt to catch fish under precise conditions and with specialized equipment (e.g., spring-fed streams and fly tackle) (Bryan, *Conflict* 45). Progression through these stages is as much a matter of socialization as time. One may enter a later stage, being socialized into the norms and values of later stages, early in one's involvement in the sport.

The bass and trout fishing literature offers another typology of sporting value systems which is interwoven with the typologies just reviewed. Trout and bass fishing reflect two different patterns of values and norms, and illustrate two, polar-opposite conceptions of fair play (reflected in Figure 1). On the one hand is the *democratic* view that the challenge and opportunities should be extended to as many fishers as possible. This *inclusive* approach implies that the practice of the sport by public rules has a civilizing effect on the participants (Huizinga, *Homo Ludens*). Thus, the standards of practice should remain reasonable and achievable. This view is probably behind the increasing participation in fishing in America, especially bass fishing, during the past 40 years. It justifies the substantial public expenditures on fishery improvements and access, and is both cause and effect of the interest shown by corporate capitalism in developing and producing the ever-expanding array of fishing equipment for the growing fishing public (to be discussed later). Also, this view of fishing recruits participants into the early stages of the progressive goal-orientation cited above. Additionally, the democratic view encourages various forms of competition among fishers in which the goals are external—the most and/or largest fish caught. The increasing popularity of tournament fishing promotes social competition among those pursuing the *democratic-inclusive* ideal. Public acclaim for winners, financial awards and stimulation of the fishing-equipment industry are all products of such competitions. Finally, a convenient fact which encourages the *democratic-inclusive* view of sport fishing is that the most popular prey, the largemouth bass, is found in all 50 states (Henschel 42).

Figure 1: Comparisons of Ideal-Typical Forms of Fishing

| | BASS FISHING | TROUT FISHING |
|---|---|---|
| **VALUE ORIENTATIONS** | Democratic-Inclusive | Elitist-Exclusive |
| **GOALS** | Most/biggest fish | Most difficult fish |
| **MEANS** | Technology (latest gadgets) | Craftsmanship (lightest tackle) |
| **STANDARDS OF PERFORMANCE** | Results of performance (the catch) | Quality of performance (catch & release) |
| **REWARDS** | External (displayed skills, public esteem) | Internal (self satisfaction) |
| **PARTICIPANTS** | Mass appeal | Selective appeal |
| **TECHNOLOGY** | Promoted | Resisted |

On the other hand, an *elitist-exclusive* view of sport in fishing strives to maintain standards of performance in the pursuit of fish, regardless of who is excluded. "Measure up or step aside" and find another pastime. This notion of fair play is embraced by those who have entered the later or final states of goal orientations suggested by Bryan ("Spring-Stream," *Conflict*; 1979) and Waterman (*History*). An example is trout fishing, an ancient sport whose traditions have raised its practice to a high art. Here, the goal may be to catch the trout under the most exacting conditions but not to keep it. Because many trout fishers believe that "the trout is too grand a fish to be caught only once," "catch-and-release" is a tradition currently enforced in many jurisdictions. Also, barbless hooks, reducing injury to the fish and increasing the chance of its escape, are prescribed. An officially designated "trout stream" will allow only artificial lures (generally hand-tied), and perhaps only barbless hooks, as well as strict limits to numbers/sizes of trout to be retained. Some streams have sections where "one-only" or "catch-and-release" are enforced. The informal rules may also prescribe that time spent playing the hooked fish be limited to reduce the stress on its system and thus increase its chances for recovery after release. These forms of self-control exercised by trout fishers are sources of internal, self-observed achievement. The rewards for practice of the *elitist* view are the more private rewards of self-satisfaction. The self-restraint of the fisher and the difficulty of the conditions cannot be put on a scale or photographed. Finally, the trout is found only in limited areas, thus excluding many from its pursuit.

It must be admitted that while the *elitist* version of fair play is best illustrated from among the ranks of fly-trout fishers, most trout fishers do not subscribe to the elitist conception. There are some 18 million trout fishers in the U.S., most of whom use either live bait or commercial lures (Hope). Thus, most trout fishers would largely fall in the democratic camp rather than the elitist camp, and an appropriate distinction might be "those who fish for trout" as opposed to "trout fishers." Part of the elitism is holding the technological advantage in check, purposefully imposing difficulties (Hope 163-64).[3]

> A fish will often ignore or spit out a trout fly as soon as it senses the false feel of feather, but with live bait, a strike and swallow by the trout are virtually guaranteed...unlike the small, single-hook fly, a typical lure may be equipped with four to nine hooks along its three-inch length. And because the factory lures or live bait weigh between 75 and 300 times more than the average trout fly, it is far easier to cast them with distance and accuracy. The fly-fisherman, because of his choice of a tiny lure that commonly weighs less than .01 ounce, must use an elaborate and perfectly timed series of motions to achieve a cast of even 30 feet.... This forces him to wade close to his skittish prey and, if he hooks a one-pound trout, to work it to the net with infinite patience and delicacy to prevent his gossamerlike leader from breaking. But the dedicated fly-fisherman exults in these difficulties. The difference between this kind of fishing and any other...is precisely that of experiencing the elegance and grace and ritual of the Japanese tea ceremony...versus dunking a tea bag into a plastic cup of tepid water. (Hope 163)

In sum, the sport in the *elitist* version exists between the fisher and the fish/nature. In the *democratic* notion, the sport has shifted to exist between or among fishers, i.e., who can catch the most or biggest fish; hence, there is an accepted emphasis on technology because it becomes the means to attain the sport objective.

## TECHNOLOGY IN FISHING

It is impossible to detail the history of all innovations in fishing, first because such innovations are so extensive, and second, because much of the technological change is lost in antiquity. It is also impossible to detail the full breadth of the recent innovations (Circle 49). Thus, the focus is largely restricted to the major components of fishing tackle (i.e., hooks, lures, line, rods and reels), with some attention to "high tech."

Hooks have not appreciably changed, except for alloys, since about 1920. By then, hook penetration had been perfected by the eagle claw bend, and hooks were being machine-made and tempered. Historically, hooks had been hand-crafted, without benefit of superior alloys, and hand-tempered, often producing hooks either too brittle or too soft. Prehistorically, hooks had been made from shell, lithic materials, bone, bronze and even wood (Gabrielson 106-11).

The evolution of artificial lures, at least as old as ancient Greek culture (Rundell), has recently resulted in soft-bodied, anatomically accurate imitations of fishes, minnows, frogs, crayfish and so on. Spray-on lure coatings have an appealing taste to fish, inducing them to try to swallow the lure, giving the angler more time to set the hook before the lure is expelled (Circle 49). Most recently, artificial minnows and fingerling fish are available, consisting of 70 percent real fish. Lure selection and use can now be determined through boat-mounted computers:

> More than 750,000 lure selections by type, color and type of retrieve to be used with the lures which are programmed into the computer. The angler enters all variables, such as the season of the year, weather, wind and other pertinent information. The device then provides a readout on what lure combination should be most productive and how to fish the lure. (Henschel 42)

Lines have evolved from natural materials (e.g., horse-hair, vines, silk threads, strips of intestine) to synthetics (nylon), but limits to strength have been established to maintain the challenge. The synthetic materials reduce the costs and the care required to maintain the line.

Rods evolved from cumbersome sapling poles to split bamboo. Bamboo was partly replaced by metal rods, though the greatest advance was the use of fiberglass shortly after World War II (Gabrielson 119-24). Today, graphite and boron rods produce lighter weight, greater sensitivity to strikes, longer casts and improved hooking potential (Henschel 42).

The first practical reels, occurring about 1830 (Gabrielson 116-19), were hand-crafted and thus had few or no interchangeable parts. Innovations introduced within the last decade include a liquid-crystal-display (LCD), microcomputerized, baitcasting reel which gives a readout of casting distance or amount of line out for deep jigging and trolling, and a readout of how much line is left on the spool; it beeps every second to assist in controlling speed of lure retrieval or estimating how deep one's lure is sinking, and has magnetic control to eliminate backlash (Circle 49).

Other recent innovations assist the fisher in various ways. For example, depth finders provide accurate images of submerged terrain, i.e., likely fish habitats. Sonar units locate fish. A microcomputer depthsounder combines fish markers and depth finders to read fish and terrain down to 480 feet. It registers at speeds in excess of 75 miles per hour and beeps an operator-alert to fish or underwater hazards (Circle 48). Also available are pH meters for determining the pH levels (acidity) which influence location and feeding habits of various fish species. Water thermometers, adjustable for depth, and devices for measuring the oxygen content of water are now commonly used by serious bass fishers (Henschel 42).

Just out in 1993 is a unit which combines the fish finding features listed above with a navigational system:

> The Humminbird GPS Navigational System uses advanced global positioning satellite technology to actually show where a boat is located and in what direction it is headed.
>
> With the push of a button, this navigational system, with built-in maps, uniquely determines a boat's exact location and draws a map, positioning the craft on it and tracking the precise course history. Maps cover all inland waterways and lakes as well as coastal areas from the Caribbean to Nova Scotia, and from Baja California peninsula to Canada's Vancouver Island....
>
> Utilizing the U.S. Department of Defense $10 billion, all-weather, 24-hour a day, worldwide navigation system, the

Humminbird GPS Navigational System can lock onto satellite signals and compute latitude, longitude, TDs, altitude, course and speed—and precisely update it all once every second. (Wooldridge 62)

The technological developments reviewed are primarily applicable to bass fishing, are not appropriate to trout habitats, and have few comparable parallels in trout fishing. While fly rods and reels can take advantage of new materials, the designs remain unchanged, and some artifacts, such as flies, are still hand-tied (Hope). In essence, it is craftsmanship in trout fishing versus technology in bass fishing.

### IMPACT OF TECHNOLOGY ON PARTICIPATION

Technological developments have paralleled increased participation in fishing. National statistics for those holding fishing licenses (maintained since 1933) show that between 1933 and 1980, numbers of license holders increased five times faster than the rate of growth of the U.S. population as a whole (U.S. Department of Commerce, 1960; 1983).[4]

Technology permits an increasing number of participants for at least three reasons, all compatible with the democratic notion of fair play. First, the mass-produced technology has lowered the cost of equipment. Second, some of the technology has democratized necessary skill by reducing the difficulty of proper equipment use (e.g., the spinning reel virtually eliminated backlash in casting and thus the necessity of an "educated thumb" to act as a drag on line being cast), increasing access to fish (e.g., fish locators), traveling to their habitat (off-road vehicles) and approaching them in their habitat (e.g., bass boats, outboard motors). Third, both public and private agencies supply "techknowledge" to facilitate sport fishing by constructing/ maintaining fish habitats, sponsoring stocking/breeding programs, conducting research into fish behavior and nutritional requirements, promoting sport tourism, and so on.

Also contributing to and reflecting increased participation are the various fishing organizations, themselves partially the products of increased technology.[5] Primary among them is B.A.S.S., founded in 1968. B.A.S.S., the largest fishing organization in the world, has more than 400,000 members with 1,600 affiliated chapters (Henschel 43), and its own bimonthly publication, *Bass Master Magazine*. On the other hand, Trout

Unlimited has some 15,000 members and 176 chapters (Sosin 460), a market with much less profit potential.

B.A.S.S. has stimulated interest in fishing by sponsoring tournaments, giving rise to professional sport angling.[6] While trout fishers embracing the elitist conception of fair play would deplore such tournaments, they appeal to the democratic definitions of fair play as well as to the commercial interests of the tournament sponsors, resort areas where they are held, and the manufacturers of fishing tackle. Such tournaments have democratic appeal because the equipment used is within the financial means of the ardent followers of the sport (Henschel 43). Economy of scale further reduces the costs to gadget-happy fishers who endlessly seek to increase success in their pursuit of the largemouth bass. It is obvious that fishing tournaments do not promote fair play beyond Waterman's (*History*) first and second categories.

While the evidence examined so far suggests that technological developments increased participation in fishing, it still remains to determine what is the potential impact of fishing technology on conceptions of fair play.

### IMPACTS OF TECHNOLOGY ON FAIR PLAY

Technology enhances success in two directions. First, much of the tackle developed is easier to use and less skill-oriented. Second, fishing electronics, e.g., pH meters and sonars, can accurately predict where the fish are and where they will (or at least will not) be biting, thereby removing much of the uncertainty inherent in fishing. Thus, "innovative research and high technology have...resulted in products that give today's fisherman a better angling edge" (Circle 49).

The greater issue is how this "better angling edge" has affected the concept of fair play. From an elitist perspective, technology has contaminated the concept of fair play. The democratic-inclusive response to this implicit charge can be to rationalize the use of advanced fishing technology, and/or to use technology designed to impose handicaps (with the emphasis on the technology of the democratic orientation and not on the craftsmanship of the elitist orientation).

State-of-the-art angling technology can be rationalized by anthropomorphizing the fishes, depicting them as sly, cunning, crafty. For example, in addressing the often misunderstood competition in tournament fishing, Ray Scott, founder of B.A.S.S., says:

competitive fishing...does not pit man against man.... This is a game of man's skill against the almost unpredictable actions and activities of a very special fish, namely the largemouth bass. (Henschel 44)

Another rationalization for using the technological advantage in fishing is the B.A.S.S. tournament's requirement that all fish caught be kept in healthy condition and released after the tournament weigh-in. This has become the standard for nearly all bass tournaments in the country (Henschel 44), and is being imitated by non-tournament bass anglers as well (Williams, "Fishing" 90).

Certainly, this practice is ecologically sound since some tournaments may catch a significant part of the bass population for any single body of water, and it avoids the bad press which follows in the wake of any fishing tournament when anglers are seen carrying around heavy stringers of dead fish carcasses (Weiss 35).

To compensate for the technological advantage, democratic anglers may also impose technologically-designed "handicaps." Apparently, one of the more popular handicaps is the use of ultra-light tackle. In 1980, the International Game Fish Association established world record, freshwater fish categories based on line size (i.e., 4, 8, 12, 16, 20 and 30 pound test) (Price). New world record line categories make world records available to many more anglers, and ultra-light equipment would seem to afford fish a greater sporting chance for escape before being landed, especially since ultra-light equipment may dictate that the fish be played longer and more skillfully before being landed. However, longer play over-stresses the fish and reduces its chances for recovery if released after being landed. The sport is not the fish but the equipment in this case.

Thus, the impacts of technology on fair play depend upon the ideal-typical position. The elitist-exclusive position resists the technological advantage and exercises the handicaps occurring through the necessary skill/performance levels. The democratic-inclusive position rationalizes the technological advantage by anthropomorphizing the fish or utilizing technology with built-in handicaps. And ultimately, the accommodation or rejection of any technological advantage is only a reflection of the ideological conflicts between the democratic and elitist positions.

## CONFLICTS BETWEEN DEMOCRATIC
## AND ELITIST CONCEPTIONS OF FAIR PLAY

Supporters of the democratic conception of fair play have a voice in the magazine published by B.A.S.S., *Bass Master*, as well as a significant proportion of the product ads and articles in the popular outdoor press (e.g., *Field and Stream, Outdoor Life, Sports Afield*). The democratic view seems to ignore (or sees as non-threatening) the elitist conception. On the other hand, the elitists have their own perspective which repeatedly examines and compares the democratic-inclusive with their own value and normative system. "The opinion leaders of this angling fraternity are the highly visible outdoor writers, the articulators of the specialist's value system" (Bryan, "Leisure" 183). The following analysis offers a flavor of the invidious comparisons drawn between the two conceptions of fair play by the "opinion leaders."

While fishing tournaments have been credited with making knowledge and information public that had previously been coveted by jealous, successful anglers (democratic ideal) (Henschel 44), they have also been criticized as debasing fair play (elitist ideal). During their 20-year history, tournaments have gone from casual socializing to a multi-million-dollar industry, being criticized not so much for what they do to fish as for what they do to anglers (Williams, "Fishing" 82, 84):

> ...Americans are forgetting what fish are, and...this lapse of memory, more than anything, has been responsible for the boom in fishing tournaments. As wild...creatures reflecting the wildness and beauty of the places in which they abide, fish no longer count for much. What we have lost is what...George Bird Grinnell, in his old sporting weekly *Forest and Stream*, used to call "a refined taste in natural objects." This is why the Bass Research Foundation can underwrite a project to develop an artificial fish called the "meanmouth" by crossbreeding smallmouths and largemouths. This is why...where almost all trout fishing is "put-and-take"—it becomes increasingly difficult even to pretend that the hatchery-reared...rainbows are wild. (Williams, "Fishing" 93)

The Bass Research Foundation "has underwritten recreational fishing projects with funds of more than $ 1,500,000" (Henschel 44), and seems more devoted to enhancing the entertainment of fishing than the sport of fishing. Certainly, the "put-and-take" practice developed in trout fishing has an unsettling analogy to the carnival fish pond or "shooting fish in a barrel," though public expenditures involved can only be justified by a democratic definition of fair play. Hatchery trout are much less selective and efficient feeders than wild trout. Icthyologists have even anthropomorphized hatchery fish as "dumb," "foolish," "stupid" and "very stupid," and fly fishers are not flattered when such "man-made" fish take their hand-tied flies (Hope 166-67) (see also Weiss 35.

The conflict between these two ideal-typical perspectives will probably continue unabated. While the democratic-inclusive emphasis on technology is consistent with the popular acceptance of technology as a blessing in the general culture, the elitist-exclusive fraternity will continue in its role as a Cassandra, broadcasting warnings to the converted and unconverted alike.

## CONCLUSIONS

Our society, in part because of its technological lifestyle, is criticized as being fast-paced (c.f. Linder). This is reflected as well in the growing sport of fishing. There has been a compression of time made possible by fishing technology. Fish can be located and more fish caught in a shorter time than was possible when our vision stopped at the water's surface. We can now locate fish and quickly determine why they refuse to feed (pH, oxygen, temperature), minimizing effort and "wasted time." Given the technology, one can now buy what once had to be earned or learned only through an investment of time and awareness of nature. (See chapter 10 for more on sport as commodity.)

The technology of fishing is threatening to become more important than the natural setting, breeding "discontent in all the fishermen who used to think they were happy soaking up sun on the bank and doughballs in the creek" (Williams, "Fishing" 93). Writing in the 1940s, Aldo Leopold said:

> I have the impression that the American sportsman is puzzled; he doesn't understand what is happening to him. Bigger and better gadgets are good for industry, so why not for outdoor recreation? It has not dawned on him that outdoor recreations are essentially, primitive, atavistic; that their value is contrast-value; that excessive mechanization destroys contrasts by moving the factory to the woods or to the marsh.

The sportsman has no leaders to tell him what is wrong. The sporting press no longer represents sport; it has turned billboard for the gadgeteer. (qtd. in Williams, "Fishing" 93)

Those who guard the standards and practices of fair play are faced with two alternatives. If they choose to accept the technological changes in their sport, they must maintain eternal vigilance against the debasement of achievements when aided by technology. Standards of fair play must be adjusted continually. The other alternative is to reject almost all technological changes.

The concept of fair play or sportsmanship is not some unidimensional variable that is either present or absent in an activity. Rather, it varies in quality and quantity, and these subtleties must never be overlooked.

# Chapter Five

## Great Lakes and Deep Sea Sport Fishing: Hooked on Technology

### INTRODUCTION

In this chapter I examine the issues raised in the last chapter which argued that technology is responded to in divergent ways by various forms of freshwater sport fishing. Bass fishing encourages technological changes which improve the chances of the widest audience being able to participate and succeed when fishing for the largemouth bass. Trout fishing, on the other hand, tends to scorn most technological innovations and retains hallowed techniques and standards in its practice.

In contrast, much of the sport fishing conducted on the deep seas and Great Lakes has no choice but to accept and utilize relatively recent technology in order to pursue the fishes of interest. The fisher becomes part of a team whose other members are typically professional guides and boatmen. The team must cooperate to travel to, find, lure, hook and land the fishes from those watery environments. The standards of fair play for the prey which involve so much more than just the efforts of the fisher are of special interest here. Their history, enforcement and consequences are all part of the record compiled here which sheds light on humankind's continual quest for games to challenge our physical and mental skills. The sport, recreation, competitions of tournaments found in this form of fishing are only possible because of the technology.

The Great Lakes and oceans were fished in earlier days; however, only the smaller fishes of those marine environments were pursued because the angling technology for capturing larger fish for sport was not developed until this century. When larger fish in the Great Lakes such as the salmon were pursued, clubs and spears were the common means of taking them (Parsons 16). Along the ocean shores, larger fish such as the sea bass, devil-fish (manta rays) and tarpon were sought with lance and harpoons from "small oar- or sail-powered dories..." (G. Reiger, *Profiles* 46).

With the development of the requisite technology which enables the larger fishes to be pursued, the modern fisher has become dependent on these mechanical aids. He cannot reject them. The use of such technology places deep sea and Great Lakes fishing in the sports category requiring other human uses of machines to carry on the activity: auto racing, airplane racing, etc.

## QUESTIONS OF FAIR PLAY IN FISHING

Sportsmanship is conduct according to rules of fair play/chase which specify acceptable means of pursuit of the goal, in the current case, fishes. These rules specify what tools are to be used, how they are to be used, how the prey is to be treated once captured, and how much assistance, if any, is permitted to the fisher. In deep sea and Great Lakes fishing the required tools and assistance in their use raise grave issues about the meaning of "fair sport."

Fishing is one of the so-called "blood" sports, in that a living organism is pursued and captured and often killed in order for the sportsperson to achieve the goal. There are exceptions to this definition, however. Some forms of sport fishing encourage catch-and-release among fishers. The caught prey lives to be captured, perhaps, another day. This is a principle found and enforced in various fishing competitions: bass, trout, deep sea billfishing, etc.

One rationalization for such a sport where the taking of life is involved is that the prey species is good food as well as manifesting other sporting qualities. In deep sea fishing, however, the prey is often several times larger than the fisher and not at all of interest as food. This puts this form of fishing in the category with big game trophy hunting where the game is not necessarily eaten but immortalized by some symbol of its life: head, horns, antlers, skin.

In fishing, knowledge of habitat, bait, behaviors of fish, tackle use, are all humanly achievable. But what if one or more of these components of fishing lore is compressed or substituted when pursuing and capturing a fish? Has "fair play" been diluted or debased if knowledge of habitat, food and behavior of the fish is possessed and displayed by a fishing guide for the benefit of the fisher rather than being possessed by the fisher himself (almost always true in deep sea and great lakes charter boat fishing excursions)? If the fisher uses mechanical devices to place his baits/lures (outriggers, downriggers) at distances away and depths and move his baits/lures at speeds not achievable by other means (use of inboard motor cruisers to troll) attract fish, is he ignoring and overcoming the very handicaps which produce the sport? If he uses depth-finders to chart the hidden contours of oceans and Great Lakes and other devices to measure temperatures, etc., is he cheating by not paying his dues of experience and exposure to the vagaries of luck which true sportsmen willingly endure? If he, in other words, compresses the experience in time and space by various technological devices, is he elevating the certainty of success to unsporting levels?

In many forms of deep sea and Great Lakes fishing, the fishing boat trolls the bait along behind and beside it, and only after the fish takes the bait/lure does the fisher enter the process of capture. The sport is restricted to playing/fighting the fish after it is hooked. The extent to which help is provided the fisher and considered legitimate is illustrated in the following ad of a Lake Michigan charter boat service:

We'll take you where the action is! During the hot summer months the cool water loving lunkers you're going after seek water temperatures of 40 to 57 degrees. That means you'll be fishing up to ten miles out. You need power to take you out there in a hurry, and a skillful crew with the most up-to-date equipment available to help you locate the school once you arrive.

Every NBC Charter boat is equipped with Electronic Fish Finders that pinpoint schools of fish...and the exact depth they're swimming. Temperature downriggers take your line to the right depth and temperature reading to help assure you're fishing in the ideal thermocline for active, aggressive feeding, i.e., the prime "striking" zone. In addition, every NBC boat is equipped with ship-to-shore radio. They keep us in contact with each other as we seek out schools of fish and report the "honey holes" where the big ones are really biting. We also monitor the Coast Guard weather reports. Should the weather forecast suddenly turn rough, we can get a head start on approaching bad weather and beat the on-coming weather back to shore.

Imagine yourself doing Battle with a 10 to 25 pound Coho, Steelhead, Chinook, German Brown, or Lake Trout! These lusty fighters astound even veteran fishermen with their sky-bursting leaps and reel-stripping runs. And even after 30 minutes to occasionally over an hour of fatiguing play, they still have enough energy left to escape the landing net unless you've got an experienced captain to lend a hand at the moment of truth.

NBC Charter Service was created to make these thrills available to people like you. People who want to enjoy all the excitement of big game fishing without the expense and years of apprenticeship it takes to hook that first big one on your own. Our three boat NBC fleet has the experience, equipment and skill it takes to get you out to where the fishing is best so that you can hook a "scrapper" the first time out. (New Buffalo Charter Service)

What we see in this ad is the assertion that the modern sportsperson need not do anything but avail himself of the technology of modern boats and the techknowledge of boat crews to reach the ultimate end of the sport fishing experience—finding, hooking and landing the game fish. This approach to sport fishing is typical of both Great Lakes and deep sea fishing. The fisher has no option but to either charter such a package of technology and techknowledge or own and maintain the package if his financial circumstances permit. (Of course, the options exist to fish from piers, on shores, in the surf, etc. These options do not remove these forms of fishing from the tradition of Izaak Walton.)

Another complicating factor in attempts to practice fair play in fishing is found among the practices of catch-and-release which are observed by many fresh-water fishers for trout, bass during tournaments, and salt-water tournaments seeking the various bill fishes: sword, marlin, etc. It seems to be one of the charms of fishing that the prey can be released. However, some sport species are poor candidates for release because of their poor survival rate after capture: "...lake trout, coho salmon, and chinook (king) salmon...winched from extremely deep, cold water to the warm surface by means of downriggers" (Weiss 35). They suffer the effects of temperature changes, lactic acid buildup in muscles from struggling to escape, etc. Tuna caught during tournaments are considered poor candidates for survival unless they are "towed about" to give them time to recover. Few tournament boat captains are willing to spend the time (Williams, "Hiking" 85).

## EFFECTS OF TECHNOLOGY AND TECHKNOWLEDGE
## ON BIG GAME FISHING

Big game fishing is virtually impossible without the use of the latest achievements in human invention and investigation. When the fisher is taken miles off shore on an inboard cruiser at least 31 feet long (inboard motors are preferred because their lower mounting creates greater stability in the motions of the boat, avoids clutter/obstacles on the stern where fish are played and over which they are landed), he is normally just a passenger as the captain/owner of the boat uses navigational equipment to reach the fishing grounds. The boat is a powered fishing platform which serves various functions which a landborn fisher would produce for himself: the boat trolls the baits, as many as five at a time, at speeds experience shows are effective to lure the prey. Some game fish (i.e., some varieties of tuna) are even attracted by the motion, noise, commotion created by the boat. Other varieties are frightened by the boat and all possible care is exercised to minimize these effects. The fishing lines are attached to rods which are inserted in holders. Two out of the five possible baits are on lines attached to outriggers, which are long poles extending perpendicularly starboard and port from the trolling boat. The lines are clipped to pulleys which are hoisted up onto the ends of the outriggers which tow the baits behind and to the sides of the boat. When a fish strikes a bait, the line is pulled free of the clip on the end of the outrigger and falls back behind the boat, giving the fisher time to take up or be given his rod by the boat's crew. He then "fights"/plays the fish, perhaps with the aid of a swiveling "fighting chair" which is fastened to the boat. The fisher is harnessed in the chair, which supports the fisher's physique in various critical locations as he attempts to tire and land the fish. The boat's captain maneuvers the boat in helpful ways to the fisher: slowing to reduce the runout of line from the fishing reel, turning and following the fleeing fish so that slack can be retrieved by the fisher, etc. The boat's crew aids the fisher by offering advice if asked, adjusting the fighting chair if necessary, cooling the reel and spooled line with sea water, gaffing the fish when alongside the boat and landing/releasing it at the end of the "battle."

Another example of technology increasing and even creating sport is found in recent developments in genetic research with fishes as well as other areas of research. The Great Lakes sport fisheries have been restored to heights perhaps never before seen. This has been accomplished by a combination of pollution abatement programs enforced for industries along the lakes and development of an effective lampricide which has stemmed the plague of the sea lamprey which invaded the Great Lakes and decimated the sport fish species. Also, the introduction of the coho and chinook salmons in the 1960s to Lake Michigan and their resounding successes (from the fishers' perspective) suggested the possibilities of these great freshwater reservoirs as sport fisheries.

Another example is found in a joint project of Michigan State University and the Michigan Department of Natural Resources to introduce "...huge, sterile chinook salmon" into Lake Michigan to enhance fishing opportunities for one of the state's prime resources—sportsmen:

> These fish—scientifically called triploids—have three sets of chromosomes instead of the normal two as the result of exposing fertilized eggs to high temperature. Since these fish do not reach sexual maturity, the energy they would put into sperm or egg production and spawning is converted into growth, and triploid fish can be expected to live longer and grow larger than their sexually mature brethren.

> According to (the researcher), "Triploid chinook will not be expected to return to the streams during the spawning runs, but will stay in the lake. Those that survive angling and natural mortality factors should continue to put their energy into growth, resulting in bigger fish over time." (Schultz 75)

An additional application of technology, although slightly less exotic, has been carried out by Indiana which brought Skamania steelhead trout from Washington State for release off the Indiana shore of Lake Michigan. This variety is ideal for that habitat because the species remains throughout the summer in the vicinity of the Indiana shore, grows to large size and struggles fiercely when hooked (Schultz 78). Again we have a case where techknowledge creates a sporting opportunity where none existed before.

## ESTABLISHING STANDARDS OF FAIR PLAY
## IN THE FACE OF MASSIVE TECHNOLOGY

The spread of deep sea fishing among wealthy sportsmen, the establishment of fishing clubs in various fishing centers of the world, and the varying standards of performance and equipment used in the developing competitions among fishers to catch the biggest specimens of various salt-water game fish stimulated the formation of the International Game Fishing Association in 1939. Its goals were to standardize equipment requirements and practices used in seeking record catches and to "serve as a central processing center for world record catch data" (I.G.F.A. 12). Their current list of goals includes nine objectives:

1. Encourage the study of game fish angling in all its aspects.
2. Work for the preservation of species and habitats.
3. Compile and distribute game fish information to all interested publics.
4. Ensure recreational anglers' interests are represented at meetings dealing with the future of angling sport.
5. Stimulate game fish seminars and symposiums with assistance and participation.
6. Support various programs collecting scientific data on game fish species.
7. Maintain and promote fair, uniform, and ethical international angling regulations, and compile and maintain world record data for game fish caught according to these regulations.
8. Develop reference library on game fish, angling sport, etc.
9. Develop international history of game fishing (I.G.F.A. 12).

The fisherman's part in the process of big game fishing is combining his brains and brawn to manage his tackle when the fish is hooked. However, acknowledging the role of the tackle in the process further clarifies the technological aids in this recreation. In the words of one renowned expert:

It's a grand and glorious feeling to be photographed standing alongside a fish larger, maybe by several times, than its beaming victor.... Casually, often very casually, the tackle used is held in one hand as the shutter clicks. The tackle is included only to indicate the victorious fisherman among the rest of the admiring party. If the position of prominence were where it belonged, the tackle would be on a plush pillow in the center of the picture next to the fish and the angler positioned over to one side—barely among those present.

Why this reversal of importance? Because the fisherman did not outfight the fish now hanging on the scaffold. The tackle did most of the work. All the fisherman did was to handle the tackle, and he had to go his limit to accomplish that. The man does not live that can whip his weight in fish without the help of tackle. Put a man on a flat deck without railings or toe holds and with a 30-foot rope hook him a marlin or broadbill his equal in weight. He would be pulled off that deck and through the water so fast that he would not even drown—he would be pulled apart (Major 86).

Major supported his contention with evidence from an experiment in which he found that a 60 lb. tuna could travel at 44 m.p.h. while exerting 78 lbs. of "pull" (87). This datum can be interpreted several ways. It underlines man's minor contribution to the process, and spotlights the potency of the big game fish as an object of prey. Hence, he directs the fisher to pay careful attention to the balance of the various components of the crucial tackle. Techknowledge has accumulated to reveal how rod, line, reel and terminal tackle must be matched for strength and performance.

### GREAT LAKES SPORT FISHING AND TECHNOLOGY
Sport fishing in the Great Lakes differs significantly from deep sea salt water fishing. Sport fishes in salt water are primarily surface feeders who are sought and lured with surface baits which can be watched visually almost at all times. On the other hand, sport fishes in the Great Lakes are not surface feeders, and the hunt for them must be conducted by other than direct visual means. Thus, the Great Lakes have been the arena in which some other technological developments have emerged. A recent treatise on techniques for use of the downrigger contends:

Downriggers were created by Great Lakes inventors because salmonids imported from the Pacific and Atlantic Oceans suspended in middle water where they could not be taken with long weighted lines. A weighted line is reasonably efficient in upper waters to 20 feet. It's also reasonably efficient when bumping bottom in lower waters. It's horribly inefficient, because of line bellying and the effect of water pressures and currents, at middle depths. It was generally recognized that more precise trolling presentation to fish's mouths was needed at all water depths. The downrigger satisfies this need. (Olson 60-61)

However, the downrigger is just one device among a system of devices for locating and catching sport fishes in the Great Lakes. The downrigger only delivers the last requirement for catching fish: presenting the lure at the right depth. Before this stage, the fisher must use the techknowledge that:

> ...fish usually seek habitat by temperature preference,...the habitat can be located with a thermometer,...the fish can be located within the temperature habitat with sonar, and...(then) they can be caught on lures presented by a downrigger. (Olson 122)

What this expert is contending is that fishing for the salmonids depends on the skilled use of these devices in addition to the power boat which trolls the lures held by the downriggers at speeds achievable no other way. In short, sport *with* this technology or no sport at all.

Olson (17-18) supports the case being argued here with his description of a fully equipped charter fishing boat in Lake Michigan. His details provide a list of the technological devices a fisher on those waters must master:

> The "Sue-Ya" is a modified deep-V bow, a 10-foot beam, and twin 160 engines. It's equipped with a Modar marine-band radio, a Bear Cat CB, a commercial graph-type sonar (Kevin-Hughes) made in England for ocean use, Plath outriggers and downriggers, a Grizzly trolling indicator, and a hand-held Weller thermometer...(The captain) uses Eagle Claw 9-foot rods equipped with Penn 309 reels filled with 12-pound-test line on his starboard downriggers. At port he has an Eagle Claw Powerlight 8-foot rod equipped with an Ambassador 700 reel filled with 12-pound-test line and a Shakespeare Wonderrod equipped with a Penn Peer 209 and 15-pound-test line. He used Powerlights on the outriggers. (17-18)

## SUMMARY AND CONCLUSIONS

In an affluent society, experience becomes a commodity, packaged and peddled along with material luxuries.

Menlo Park, Calif. (UPI)—A new kind of business—the experience industry—has emerged to peddle slices of life to millions of Americans. The concept covers entrepreneurs selling a broad range of experience—from exotic vacations, to exercise studios, to drugs and quasi-spiritual seminars. (*Times-Courier* 1986)

When we have virtually every physical object we desire, we look to experiences. Many of us want them, however, packaged, finished and guaranteed to please. (See ch. 10 for an extended discussion of this point.)

Traditional conceptions of fishing as a gentle and genteel leisure/recreation/sport involved simple tools and skills acquired over time. When the fisher out of the traditional mold catches his intended prey, he can consider it an accomplishment. However, the fisher as sportsman is ever sensitive to the impact of his activity on the habitat and populations of prey. He is especially concerned with preserving and protecting the fish populations so that his pastime can be pursued indefinitely. On the other hand, if the fisher has purchased the experience of fishing by hiring a fishing guide/charter boat captain, he is more likely to demand a satisfying experience be delivered in return for his payment. He will more likely lose sight of any concern for fish populations because his self-image requires that he only engage in "good deals" which means: value received.

Of course, as long as government departments concerned with marine recreation continue to inject desirable fishes into marine ecosystems, the purchase of fishing experiences can continue indefinitely. There is no way to seriously contend the proposition that departments of fish, game, parks and recreation are all in the experience business at taxpayers' and license purchasers' expenses. The existence of these departments and their ever expanding programs provide ample evidence of the value choices of our population.

# Part 3

## MAN-ANIMAL
## INTERACTIONS
## AS SPORT

My personal pursuit of first-hand experience with various forms of sport hunting is "confessed" in the next two chapters. While my variety of experiences was broad, I cannot claim each was an adequate sample of that specific type of hunting. I believe, however, my field work allows me to better assess the candor and accuracy of reports of other hunters. This was my primary goal.

Kellert's categories of hunter motivations help order my reflections on my experiences shared in the following pages ("Attitudes"). Kellert discovered that four of every ten hunters ("utilitarians") were motivated primarily by the meat resulting from a successful hunt. Another four of every ten hunters ("dominionistics") were primarily motivated by the competition with self and others provided the hunter in the pursuit of trophies, the chance to use weapons, and the chance to master/capture the prey species. The remaining two of the ten hunters ("naturalists") were seeking the gestalt, the whole experience of entering the wild places and acting out the natural processes typical of carnivores. Success was defined by the total experience, not merely a trophy taken or meat in the freezer as proof of "productive leisure." I count myself among the naturalists in that my hunting forays did not regularly produce meat or trophies, but always took me to wild, beautiful places I would have not likely visited on other missions, and brought me face-to-face with interesting people in social psychological settings seldom, if ever, encountered by social scientists.

# Chapter Six     Seven Varieties of Sport Hunting

I spent a sabbatical leave participating in seven varieties of sport hunting available to the typical American hunter. I wanted to acquire some direct experience in various types of sport hunting as well as to compare and contrast these forms of hunting, their rewards, appeals, costs and general meanings which are produced by their practice.

## ORGANIZATION OF SPORT HUNTING
## IN ENGLAND (SCOTLAND)

Humans continue to hunt for animals, either as an economic necessity or as a means of recreation. Among humans who hunt for recreation, the resulting meat is often an important side benefit. In the British Isles sport hunting has developed into a purely recreational pastime. The game animals are considered the property of the landowners on whose land they range. Hunters of the game pay a trespass fee for the right to pursue and kill the game and are allowed to keep only the "head" as a trophy. However, the game carcasses remain the property of the landowner, are disposed of on an active game market across the continent of Europe, and provide a significant source of revenue for estate owners. The persons I interviewed claimed, however, that the revenues barely paid for the costs of maintaining the game: pay of game keepers and assistants, upkeep of shooting lodges.

In other words, when a hunter travels to U.K. to shoot game, he is paying for the right to kill other humans' animal property. All that he receives is the opportunity, thrill, exercise, satisfaction, whatever, of the pursuit, stalk. The visiting hunter is usually able to find accommodations on or close to the shooting grounds, accommodations which are comfortable, convenient and which provide all the support necessary to concentrate on the sport at hand. Since the hunter does not need to worry about caring for the meat of game animals, he can invest all his non-hunting time in rest, recreation or social interaction with other hunters.

The land owners who have shooting concessions to lease find it in their self interest to maintain healthy herds, flocks, coveys, of the game birds or animals. They are able to calculate relatively precisely how many of various species may be harvested each season in order to insure adequate supplies next year. Insuring adequate game populations to attract visiting hunters may require culling deer herds of weak, diseased members or pen-rearing pheasants until they can survive on the shooting grounds on their own with daily feeding and protection from animal predators (cats, foxes, dogs, hawks) being added to their care.

The shooting rights each season are sold to the highest bidder who may use them himself or resell them to other hunters at a profit. Shooters seeking sporting opportunities may find cancellations on shooting estates during the season on short notice.

## CONDUCT OF GROUSE "ROUGH" SHOOTING IN SCOTLAND

The red grouse is a prime sporting prey in the U.K. Its season opens on August 12 ("Glorious 12th") and lasts for approximately ten weeks. In the early weeks of the season some purists eschew the sport because they claim that the grouses' feathers are not fully developed; therefore, they cannot flee with the same speed as later in the season. Thus, the shooting is not as sporting.

The grouse shooters start each "rough" shooting day by eating breakfast at their hotel or shooting lodge. They travel to the shooting estate where they meet the gamekeeper and his assistants who will be leading the shooting during the day. The keeper, assistants, dogs and shooters travel then to the grouse moors where the shooting begins around 9 A.M. at the earliest. (Earlier starting periods are ill advised because the morning mists have not lifted and tend to obscure the shooting grounds.)

Shooting and safety procedures are carefully discussed by the keeper with the hunters before the start of the shoot. The shooters are to remain in a straight line as they walk forward, roughly 35 yards apart. They are to limit themselves to a narrow arc of fire straight in front of them and are instructed how to turn to the rear to fire at grouse going away from the line. They are also urged to watch the dogs that are ranging back and forth in front of the shooting line, seeking the scents of resting grouse.

The shooters are instructed to "walk forward slowly, gentlemen," by the keeper. The line struggles to remain straight regardless of obstacles which might range from ravines, streams, bogs. Every half hour or so the keeper calls a brief halt for a rest.

As most directions on the grouse moors are up, the shooting line usually is ascending as it moves. The keeper typically directs the line toward the highest elevation of the shooting grounds during the morning shoot. When the heights are obtained, often around 1 P.M., the half-hour lunch break is called. The lunches are generally packed by the hotels where the hunters are staying and brought to the lunching site by the ponies, led by the pony-boys. The ponies are used to carry the grouse shot by the shooting party, as well as lunches and extra gear of the shooters: raingear, etc. After lunch the party often hunts over relatively level ground or on the slopes of the hills, around their circumferences. The line then gradually hunts downhill, toward the cars. The shooters, while carrying their shotguns in a hunting-alert position, have no means of assisting in maintaining their balance as they walk over the rough moors, unlike the keepers who carry shoulder-height walking sticks. By afternoon many shooters are likely to be tiring. Often someone will fall behind the line, necessitating the line to halt occasionally. I found that descending hills was very painful for my knees and I was unable to keep up on numerous occasions. More on that later.

Whenever grouse were flushed, the shooters experienced bursts of adrenaline which reenergized the walking line. After returning from the day, the hunters and their wives typically gathered in a bar or lounge in the hotel to relate the day's experiences—the successes, misses, falls, exhaustion. These revelations were tentative at first until the hunters trusted one another's probable reactions.

The shooting form just described shares many similarities with American pheasant and quail hunting when groups of hunters sweep a habitat in an organized fashion. The more classical form of British-Scottish bird hunting, pass shooting of driven pheasants, was not part of my research experiences. This form takes place on various country estates in England, Scotland and Ireland where pheasants are pen-raised and released onto the vast acreage of the typical estate. When the hunting season opens (August 12), a prototypical shooting party will occupy randomly assigned shooting stands to await the overflight of the pheasants which are driven toward the waiting line of shooters by a moving line of beaters. When the pheasants break cover and fly over the "guns," the drive is complete. The guns then move to another set of shooting points to await the next organized drive. Grouse are driven to waiting shooters in Scotland as well. This shooting sport is among the most expensive forms and is usually only affordable by the upper classes and shooting syndicates who lease shooting opportunities for their contributing members. The downed birds belong to the estate and find their way to the game markets and ultimately appear on restaurant menus all over Europe during the season.

### CONDUCT OF RED DEER STALKING IN SCOTLAND

The red deer, a biological cousin to our American elk (wapiti), range freely over the treeless hills and moors of the estates. These treeless landscapes are termed "deer forests." One reason the grouse season is before the deer season is that reducing the numbers of grouse lowers the risk that they will startle the prey when the deer are being stalked. The red deer are most often stalked during the "rut" when the stags become less cautious as they seek sexual contact with the hinds (females) and engage in physical combat with other stags competing for access to the hinds.

Stalking the red deer is a solitary rather than group event. One hunter is guided by a professional stalker on the estate in pursuit of a suitable stag to be harvested. The stalker is assisted by a younger stalker who leads the ponies (2) on the stalk. The ponies carry extra equipment and lunches, and serve to transport the harvested stag at the end of the hunt. The head stalker has to size up the hunter he is leading, his condition, his shooting skill (tested on a target before the stalk begins), as well as plan the hunt to approach a shootable stag to within certain killing range. The goal is to seek, find, approach and dispatch a stag with one shot. Those eligible for harvesting are in several categories: old stags beyond their breeding years, stags with malformed antlers whose breeding might pass on that trait to their offspring, or stags with single points on the antlers ("hummels"), rendering them more likely to inflict damage on their opponents during rutting combats.

Removing such animals from the breeding population is considered good game management. Only occasionally are "royals" (stags with six points on each antler) actually harvested. Extra costs are typically charged on such occasions.

The hunter is led by the stalker and followed by the ponies and assistant stalker into the hills, moors, with the wind in their faces, seeking the red deer. The stalker is continually using his binoculars and/or draw-tube telescope to search for stags which might be stalked to within shooting distance. The hinds are a constant *hindrance* as they typically start at the sight or scent of humans, thus acting as "early warning systems" for other members of the herd. When a stag is spotted, the stalk is planned, which might involve crawling in the direction of the stag, circling around to approach from another direction, or waiting for the stag to move in the direction of the hunters, stand up or otherwise present himself as a target.

### PERSONAL REACTIONS TO THE KILLING OF A STAG

Hunting remains a controversial recreation in human societies. Its enemies attack it on grounds that it threatens the survival of species, is cruel, encourages the dark side of human nature, and is a form of "speciesism" in which species other than humans are denied their fundamental rights of life and liberty. Being a member of the Western academic community, I witnessed, perhaps, a purer form of this opposition than other citizens. When I decided that I needed to participate in this activity in order to more fully understand its psychological appeal and the social psychological, interpersonal processes occurring between and among hunters, and between hunters and stalkers, I was especially curious as to my anticipated reactions to the death of a stag if I were successful. I found myself very calm at the moment when a stag presented himself as a target. I also calmly followed the directions of the stalker, made sure of my intended target, aimed my rifle and ended the life of the stag. Upon the almost instantaneous death of the stag, the stalker went off to bring up the ponies for transport. The author/hunter was left alone with the stag, my own thoughts and reactions and the landscape. I felt I had stumbled into a microcosm of animal "paradise" which I had violated by my act. As I approached the stag, a trio of red grouse noisily flew off, having been sharing this part of the hill with the stag and his fellows. I felt a sad peace of mind as I inspected the downed stag. I had dispatched the animal with one shot as the sporting code prescribes. I knew the carcass would be properly processed and utilized, nothing being wasted. I knew the stag was biologically inferior by human standards because of its asymmetrical antlers, thus a perceived threat to the breeding population of the herd. With this feeling of saddened satisfaction, I walked a few yards to a small waterfall where I filled my water bottle with cold, peat-flavored water, the capstone of my memories of this microcosm of paradise.

## INTERPERSONAL PROCESSES
## AMONG THE AMERICAN HUNTING PARTY

The hunting trip, during which the preceding scene took place, was a "combination hunt" which promised grouse shooting, stag stalking, salmon fishing, among other blood sports. It seemed to promise a variety of what Scotland had to offer the visiting sportsman. I approached the trip with some anxiety, wondering what the other hunters would be like, how would the group interact. The other hunters turned out to be avid "bird" hunters: quail, pheasant, ducks, geese, grouse, partridge. Only one other hunter really wanted a stag hunt (which never materialized for him during the week because of high water on a river running through the deer forest). As a result, the conditions for the grouse shooting seemed to suit the other four hunters quite well. The group shared only its collective love of bird hunting. The occupations of all but the author were quite lucrative: engineer, heart specialist, pharmacist, song-writer/publisher.

The group included two northeastern hunters and two southern hunters as well as myself. A subtle competition existed among the shooters as to the numbers of grouse they claimed having downed each day. One hunter was very sure; one hunter was somewhat certain; the other two were less inclined to claim fixed totals. One hunter seemed especially assertive in claiming his "kill" numbers. This trait never provoked open conflict within the group; however, the potential always existed.

The physical stresses of climbing the moors and walking in line were only gradually commented on as the group came to know one another. The group seemed to evolve a standard degree of confession. All would willingly admit the existence of sore feet, blisters, sore muscles. None would admit that the stresses were too rigorous. The male ego is a fragile shell when matters of physical performance in some chosen recreation are addressed. By the end of the third day, I was crippled in the knees from the descents from the hills. I could not keep up with the line on the third day as it descended the hill at the very end. I was chagrined, ashamed, saddened, frightened, wondering how the group would react to my infirmity. When I caught up with the group, not a word was said, no notice given of my infirmity.

### ATTRACTIONS OF SCOTTISH HUNTING

Why would American or other nationality hunters travel so far and pay so much ($2600 for 5 days/travel included) to hunt animals similar to those available at home? The answers are complex. First, hunting in Scotland is brightened by its association with British upper-class tastes for the past 150 years. Queen Victoria and her husband discovered the joys of Scottish sport in the 1840s and legitimized it for all those elites who derived their recreational tastes from the royal examples. In addition, the sports available there today are essentially unchanged in form and practice from their earliest renditions. Also, the sportsman can concentrate on the sports and their challenges without having to worry about accommodations or caring for the bagged game. Hunters face the physical challenges in essentially genteel surroundings with good food, hot baths, soft beds and smooth roads supporting their recreation on every side.

### A SECOND ROUND OF DEER STALKING

I returned to Scotland for another week of only deer stalking ($2200 for 5 days/travel included). This week was spent visiting various estates, with differing terrains, which offered a variety of stalking experiences. I found one of the four estates similar to the original one I discussed earlier. The moors are rolling, open, and the deer wandered back and forth across estate boundaries as driven by the wind direction or hunting pressure or some combination of these factors. Another estate had remnants of the Caledonian Forest on its premises, a habitat which offered more shelter to the deer, reducing their caloric expenditures required to maintain body heat, thus allowing the deer to grow larger. A third estate was surrounded by a "deer fence" which prevented the deer from leaving the thousands of acres of ground. This estate provided the hunter the most certainty of being led by the stalker to a successful killing of a stag. While other estates might lead the hunter to travel with his stalker from mid-morning to early evening in pursuit of a shootable stag, the fenced estate had its stalking guide handle two hunters, one in the morning and one in the afternoon. And each hunter was led to attractive heads. In short, the certainty of a successful stalk was much increased on the fenced estate.

### A SECOND INTERIOR VIEW OF THE STALKING PROCESS

During the week of stalking I experienced virtually all of the various fortunes which can befall a hunter of the red deer in Scotland. I shot a small stag on Monday on the most open estate. I returned to the same estate on Tuesday and no shootable stag came within range, all remaining on neighboring estates. The third day I went to a second estate and did not see a shootable stag all day. Thus, I had two days without success in terms of production. The fourth day I enjoyed unexpected, glorious success on the third estate. The stalker led me into range of a large, mature stag with a trophy head (set of antlers). I was permitted to shoot it and was overwhelmed by my reactions to now "owning through death" such a beautiful animal. (More on those reactions later.) The fifth and final day of stalking I went to the fenced estate, was led up to a good stag and then managed to first miss and then wound the same stag non-critically. I went from the heights of exaltation because of my almost flawless performance on Thursday to the depths of despair, self-recrimination and repetitive self-examination of what I had done to fail on Friday. The list of possible excuses grew exponentially as I reflected on my performance.

The transaction between the stalker-guide and hunter is a process of striking a bargain. The stalker undoubtedly assesses the hunter on several dimensions: shooting skill, physical stamina, attitudes about the social organization of stalking in Scotland and general demeanor as a gentleman. I discovered in conversations with stalkers regarding other members of my party who had hunted previously with these guides that some had made negative impressions on the guides. Bragging about one's hunting prowess and ill temper were sources of negative opinions. One member of my party had had great success on the open estate the previous year. He had also irritated the guide. This hunter expected great shooting in the current year with the same stalking guide. Instead, that guide led the hunter a merry chase, walking him incessantly all day and never finding a shootable stag. The hunter was so disgusted with his day that he canceled the second day on the same estate. Whether his stalker had sabotaged the day or sanctioned the irritating hunter in some other way, I cannot confirm definitely. However, what happened is consistent with what I would have predicted after my conversation with the stalking guide.

## DEVIANCE FROM THE SPORTING ETHIC

The sporting ethic of "fair chase" in hunting/shooting/stalking is both a moral and legal prescription. It is designed to keep the hunter from exercising undue advantage over the prey animal as well as countering the criticisms of nonhunters regarding the whole cultural complex of sport hunting.

In Scotland the sporting ethic is enforced by the gamekeeper guides who supervise the stalking and shooting of the hunters. The hunters are under the nominal control of the guides at all times, receiving permission regarding which animal to shoot at, when to shoot, etc. The guides (stalkers) ideally make these decisions based on knowledge of the hunter's shooting skills, and what is in the best interests of the breeding herd. The organizer of my stalking tour stressed repeatedly that the *experience* of stalking was the main prize to be won. Shooting a stag was a bonus and receiving the chance to shoot a really large stag was a rare gift which few could expect to receive. Such a gift would be a matter of incredible luck!

The organizer's audience (the hunting party) reacted variously to this homily. I took it seriously and maintained the proper attitude throughout the week of stalking. When I did have the opportunity to shoot a large stag, I was so genuinely overwhelmed by the "gift" that I awoke for two hours in the early morning of the next day and recorded my emotional reactions to my good fortune. Also, I accepted two days without seeing a shootable stag as part of the price of pursuing such a sporting activity. I told myself and several others, "If I don't know how to lose, I don't deserve to win."

At the other extreme, several members of the hunting party were keenly interested in shooting large animals and willing to bend the sporting ethic to achieve their goal. One, with previous experience on these estates, advised a new hunter to seek out a particular stalker who "knew where the really big ones were and would take you there in exchange for an appropriate tip." Before I learned of this advice, I happened to draw that stalker for the day. He expressed his disapproval of the conduct of the hunter who offered special gratuities for access to large heads. The stalker never admitted being bribed by that hunter; perhaps he was just salving his own conscience for having accepted such a bribe the previous year. In any event, as I mentioned earlier, this stalker did not produce the large head for the briber during the current year. Instead, he led that hunter a merry chase back and forth across the estate grounds without finding any stags to shoot. The hunter did not lose his faith in the stalker but canceled a return trip to that estate out of disgust for his unsuccessful day. The attitude of this American hunter seemed to be that he had not come all this distance just to enjoy pretty walks on the moors; he had come to add to his trophy room contents at home. He expressed a desire for "productive leisure." He wanted something to show for his hunting holidays. The same stalking guide told of other clients who had offered to pay for the opportunity to shoot larger stags than the game keeper deemed wise. One client, a millionaire, supposedly offered ten pounds a point (tines on the antlers) for a large stag.

In short, the ideals of the sporting ethic in stalking are frequently assaulted by reality, as in any other activity regulated by a normative system.

## PERSONAL REACTIONS TO THE TAKING
## OF A TROPHY STAG

As mentioned earlier, on my second trip to Scotland I shot a trophy stag on the fourth day. The experience and my reactions to it were surprising, revealing and perhaps generalizable. What follows are my transcribed notes which I wrote between 2 a.m. and 4 a.m. on the morning following my success. (Please excuse the stream-of-consciousness redundancies shown in my early-morning thoughts. They reflect the avalanche of reactions which tumbled forth. I have not attempted to herd them into a more linear progression at this point.)

"I shot a trophy stag, a 'royal' (12 antler points), on Glen Tanar Estate on Thursday, October 1. Eion Smith was my stalker. He was assisted by Colin. The stag was in the rut because its stomach was empty and its body fat much reduced. American hunters are led to expect that truly trophy animals will seldom be shot because the estates want such animals' genes to be spread as widely as possible among the herd. Therefore, I was much surprised that my stalker allowed me to harvest this stag; although, I was not apprised of its size before the stalk began. The stalker had observed the stag while seeking an approach to another animal. He decided we should 'have a go' at this one instead. This required crawling on hands and knees and stomach through a grazing herd of red deer. He counseled me that I would have all my life to look at the head of the stag. Therefore, I should keep my head down during our stalk. I was able to control my curiosity and did not view the stag until just before I was called upon to shoot it.

"After the stalk was over and the stag was down, I asked the stalker why I was allowed to shoot this one. He offered several reasons: the stag had no better head this year than it had last year (he had seen it previously). He was always interested in harvesting the heaviest animals for the estate to sell on the venison market. He was concerned about the reputation of the estate for producing large animals. The stag was hanging out near the boundary of another estate whose owner tended to shoot red deer as crop marauders (threatening his turnip crop) regardless of the size of their heads. Therefore, the stalker was concerned that this stag would suffer such an ignoble death. I suspect (and fervently hope) that the stalker had found my interest in stalking in all of its historical, natural history, and sporting aspects as validation of my worthiness to take and appreciate such an noble animal. During the day we had discussed the literature of stalking and he quoted Sir Hugh Fraser (a Victorian-era author on deer stalking) to the effect that the main joy of stalking was not the stalk or the kill but the places to which stalking brings us that we would otherwise not visit. That struck a special fancy with me! Also, I believe I executed an almost perfect stalk in my role as a guided 'rifle.' I followed directions explicitly, crawling when signaled, stopping when he did, keeping my head down and overcoming the minor crisis of my rifle misfiring when I was called upon to shoot. Also, I made a killing shot. My stalker said the stag never heard the shot, dying instantly. In short, I did everything in this instance a skilled hunter should do, without error.

"A trophy comes to one who subscribes to the sporting code. it is an overwhelming gift which the recipient feels unworthy of receiving-not earned, not worthy. The hunter also experiences reverence for the death of the stag and sadness that such magnificence must end, except through its offspring.

"People in my party were extremely generous in their congratulations. I believe they were worried that my two previous days of seeing nothing would wound my male ego if my bad luck continued. I confess my own secret competitiveness as I furtively looked at other stag heads taken by the party, comparing them, worrying slightly that the last day might produce a better head. The wives of the other hunters were glad for me but still bittersweet as their husbands' own successes were diminished by mine. My stalking partner for the next day told his wife that he had achieved what he had come for, shooting a 'royal' and he was going to let me shoot all I wanted on Glen Dye the next day. (If Glen Dye is so easy, is it valuable?)

"What is a trophy worth? What makes it valuable? Rarity? Feelings it evokes in the hunter? Joy and gratitude that it has elevated the hunter in stature in the eyes of the hunting fraternity? Religious feelings of 'gift of grace'—salvation, eternal life—undeserved, such a wonderful gift for such an unworthy one? I do not feel worthy of this trophy! Is this a typical reaction? My stalker, Eion, described 'my stag' as 'a trophy of a lifetime.' Did I under reward him (gratuity) for the honor he conferred on me by allowing me to take on the responsibility of ending the life of this stag and becoming responsible for preserving the stored value and magnificence of its beauty? I can anticipate the joy it will give me whenever I look upon it in the future! The head—it belongs to me—*or do I belong to it*? I have the strange sensation that I have been assigned the duty of the caretaking of a monument to the sport of red deer stalking in Scotland. My trophy demonstrates what the sport is capable of producing. At this moment I feel there is no reason to continue in this sport—I have accomplished all that I can achieve in it!

"What to do with the trophy? Eion Smith, my stalker, commented regarding taxidermy that 'more than life goes out of a stag at its death. Most taxidermy is a travesty of its life. The head is the most tangible mark of its life.'

"These notes are being written between 2 and 4 a.m. I mention this because I woke up and cannot sleep as I review the events of the stalk. I trusted my stalker completely and became an instrument of his will and direction. I did not ask him 'how big is the stag?' I tried to give him (Eion) a good hunt by being a classic good sport—polite, alert, obedient, appreciative, competent. This was a mountaintop experience in my life—I have become engulfed in something greater than myself. I have become part of the ages of sportsmen who pursue the red stag and win. In so doing, I have received the obligation of showing reverence for an object whose value lies in its capacity to inspire awe. It is like finding some rare object you feel is too important to own privately. My obligation is to share it with other worshippers. This stag head truly displays the attributes of what Durkheim calls a 'sacred object'—that which is treated with ritual respect and is awe-inspiring.

"Tears of sadness and spasms of joy afflicted me as I left the hill. These questions confronted me—can the magnificence of the stag's life be preserved after his death? Taxidermy cannot bring him back to life. His head is but a one-dimensional physical remnant of the meaning of his existence! Like the Roman Wall in Britain, his head evokes past glories!

"This was a total experience—like unlocking a door, lock after lock—preparation, bad luck, behavior according to the code, acceptance by stalker of my worthiness to receive the opportunity to try the stalk, behavior afterward—no 'I feel great' or 'look at what I have done,' but calm, sober expressions of awe at what had transpired, doubts of worthiness, seeking reassurances that I had not done something selfish by removing this stag from the hill—his progeny would inherit the capacity for physical magnificence from their sire.

"This was truly a peak experience for me—a feeling that something great and wonderful had happened—not a testimony to me (although I'm delighted to be part of it) but an experience I am frightened of taking credit for. I did not use any great level of skill but was lucky (the awe-inspiring capacity of luck!). I never have understood so thoroughly as I do now what 'luck' can mean. Also, I have the self-satisfaction of doing something 'just right' in the sense of using all prior preparations to make this experience: rifle practice, skill at drawing out other people and leading them to perform as well or better than they ordinarily do, following instructions precisely. As quoted earlier, one of my fellow hunters claimed he got what he came after, a 'royal' head. I did not come after or expect a 'royal' head. It is explosively overwhelming that it happened to me. The gods of the hunt smiled on me. This is only understandable to those who assign value to trophies of the hunt."
4 a.m. October 2, Raemoir House Hotel, Banchory Kincardineshire, Scotland.

#### DO-IT-YOURSELF HUNTING IN THE WILDS OF CANADA
The second planned experience in my sabbatical research was a poor man's moose hunting trip ($800/7 days/travel extra) with family friends to Ontario Province of Canada. These friends had been hunting many times, moose hunting several times, and invited me to join them in a "fly-in" hunt to what was advertised as prime moose territory. This hunting trip was an economy version in the following senses: the "outfitter" arranged for us to be flown to a lake with a cabin. The cabin was equipped with lights, heating (wood stove) and refrigerator, all powered by propane. Also, the camp was provided with boats and motors. The hunters, however, had to provide their own food and cooking and conduct their own searching for the prey of the hunt. The outfitter promised to visit the hunting party two times during the week to see if anything was needed or whether a moose carcass was ready to be flown out.

Very little advice was offered by the outfitter as to where/how to find the prey. The hunters were totally responsible for that.

This kind of self-directed hunting experience requires the hunters to define, create and sustain their own reality of the hunting experience. They must decide what the rules are, how the hunt is to be conducted, how much effort will be invested in the hunting process. If the hunters decide to stay up all night and play cards, or stay in bed until after sunrise, there is no hired guide to frown at these choices. If the hunters find the anticipated conditions are not present, they are likely to redefine the situation and try to extract an altered meaning from the experience.

For example, my moose hunting party arrived at the remote wilderness lake before the hunting season opened. This was done intentionally so that they could try the fishing first. The fishing turned out to be extraordinary in quality and quantity by the definition of the hunters. Also, the hunting terrain proved to be much more difficult than anticipated. Therefore, the hunting program was redefined into a combined hunting-and-fishing program and eventually settled into a fishing-and-some-hunting program. The two more experienced hunters were also accomplished fishers and soon realized that successful fishing required much less investment of effort than successful hunting. Half-hearted attempts were made to find the signs and habitat of moose; however, the hours spent in hunting efforts were no more than 25 percent of those spent in fishing. Perhaps other hunting parties of do-it-yourselfers, confronting the same disappointing hunting conditions, would have spent more time playing cards and drinking. Members of my party were not addicted to any of the stereotypical vices commonly attributed to male hunting camps.

One member of these parties typically makes the arrangements with the seller of the wilderness hunting experience. These groups are also typically fiercely democratic, voting carefully on what food to take, when to leave, how the spoils will be divided. There may be informal leaders within the party whose roles are based on superior experience; however, even this emergent leader will preserve democratic forms by seeking consensus on the acceptance of his leadership. In my party, the two older members were the leaders and myself and the son of one of them were the "apprentices."

The chores of cooking, washing and getting water may be assigned, volunteered for or rotated among the party. The least social friction occurs, naturally, when all or most are willing to pitch in and help wherever needed. Failure to contribute appropriately provokes the expected social control mechanisms, sanctions of various kinds—verbal, interactional.

I found myself continually assessing the contributions I was making to the mechanics of the hunting party relative to other members. I felt motivated to retain a net balance rather than deficit, relative to other members. I felt this was the best way to elicit reciprocity from them toward me in the form of instruction in the mysteries and arts of fishing and hunting. I felt an indulgent, gentle superiority to those who were not contributing as much as I. I awarded myself additional honor points by "forgiving" them for their deficit balance of contributions to the general welfare relative to my own. Quite possibly recollections of my hunting partners would award me a comparable negative balance.

The game laws of Canada are to be enforced by the outfitters who provide these wilderness hunting experiences to their clients. The outfitter explained to me the hunting regulations and also revealed some typical violations. He stated that although sighting moose from boats was legal, the animals could not be shot from the boats. He admitted that 75 percent of moose are shot from boats and warned that any evidence of such behavior must be erased. Do not leave a loaded gun in a boat or any empty, fired cartridge cases. He warned that the game warden was likely to fly in to see us during our week. He was careful not to endorse any illegal activities; however, he provided the information necessary for the hunter to make his own decisions regarding "fair chase." My hunting party decided that we would shoot from the boats if given the opportunity. The party was especially careful regarding the number of fish they kept for transport home because they expected to be checked at the border. In essence, the relative fears of being caught or escaping detection seemed to dictate degrees of compliance. There was no discussion about giving animals a sporting chance to escape. In fact, the moose hunting licenses included provisions for shooting a cow (female moose) and a calf as well as two bulls, the traditional targets of moose hunters.

The thought of shooting females and the young of a prey species typically has outraged sport hunters. I felt outraged also at first. However, the rest of the party was quite interested in "productive leisure," having something to show for their trip. As the week progressed without any sightings of any variety of moose, my outrage dissipated and I became willing psychologically to take any opportunity offered.

We saw no moose, only tracks, but caught, ate and brought home a lot of fish. Because the covert goal of such economy hunts is productive leisure, the party concluded that the trip was mostly a failure. Experiencing the beautiful Canadian wilderness had not been considered as a major dividend by the party members. In short, the party was composed of three utilitarians and one nature hunter—me.

## GUIDED ELK HUNT IN IDAHO:
## SOCIAL ORGANIZATION OF GUIDED HUNTING IN AMERICA

The commercial phenomenon of guided big-game hunting in the U.S. shares several common features among its various forms. The hunter-client contracts with an outfitter-guide to provide experienced leadership in taking the client directly to the areas in which the prey species are found, to provide basic accommodations and food while in the field and to organize planned approaches to the prey species. The client bypasses the need to become familiar with the territory in which the hunt is conducted and avoids the need to look after the details of living for a period away from civilization. S/he can concentrate on the limited series of physical and mental acts required to harvest the prey species.

The opportunities for guided hunts are advertised in outdoor sporting magazines and at regional sport shows which are attended by both casual and serious shoppers for various hunting experiences/fantasies. The nature of hunting fantasies is worth exploring in some detail. What is it about various prey species which attracts hunters to invest time, money and physical efforts in their pursuit? In other words, what are hunters looking for when they put their money down?

1. Identification with famous personages of the past who have hunted particular game such as Theodore Roosevelt, Ernest Hemingway or in particular ways such as with muzzleloading arms or bows and arrows.

2. Physical challenges required to hunt particular species such as mountain goats or sheep, elk.

3. Fast and frequent action such as in water-fowl or upland game shooting when the prey species is abundant.

4. The attractiveness of the trophy displays resulting from successful hunting such as elk or moose antlers or elephant tusks.

5. The beauty of the country in which the hunting activities take place such as in the mountain wildernesses of the American West or Alaska.

6. The achievement of "doing it" by oneself without the help of a commercial guide.

These various fantasies are pursued mainly by men in various ways. Some live close enough to hunting environments that they can guide themselves in the pursuit of their prey, thus reducing/minimizing their costs. Others (most) live far from their fantasy game fields and must plan carefully for their "hunt of a life time." In many cases by the time a hunter has convinced himself that he can afford his dream hunt, he is so old that the physical demands are daunting. Also, the occupations which provide the resources to pay for these hunts are often sedentary, promoting physical deterioration as middle age approaches and passes.

Shopping for the purchase of one of these fantasies, in the pages of outdoor magazines or through attendance at a sports show, is casual browsing for most people. The outfitter selling me the elk hunt reported that of the contacts he makes at sports shows in the Eastern U.S., 30-35 percent of those who verbally claim they are going to book a hunt with him actually do so. If one gets serious about booking a hunt, he must decide almost a year in advance and make a partial payment of the fee to demonstrate his earnestness.

The outfitters/guides who advertise their services at the outdoor shows will bring videos of hunt highlights and photographs of the animals successfully harvested by their hunters. Also, they often ask previous clients in the vicinity of the shows to loan them the mounted heads resulting from successful hunts. The outfitters typically provide lists of references of satisfied customers.

My elk-hunting trip ($2300/6 days/travel extra) occurred in horrible weather (too warm and sunny) for elk sightings. Of six hunters, only three actually saw bulls and only one harvested a bull. The other two only saw males at long distances. However, four of the six hunters thought the trip was a wonderful experience, two describing it as a peak experience of their lives as they departed for home. How can the main objective be missed and the participants still be thoroughly satisfied? The beautiful habitat was one key. The other was the finely-honed, interactional skills of the outfitter. After several days of no luck with elk sightings, the pranks began. Clients who were able to take ribbing were subjected to extensive excoriations, to the delight of the onlookers. The outfitter admitted to me on the last hunting day that he worked diligently to keep spirits high when no one was seeing game and thus no one had hunting tales to share. "It can get to be very long days when no one is talking to each other beyond the bare essentials," he confessed. So, he looks for the one or few with whom he can engage in playful aggression and then commences the entertainment. The results were almost totally positive. Everyone remained in good spirits and the majority did not blame the outfitter in any way for the poor hunting results. What is an outfitter to do when he has a camp full of hunters booked and they experience a long period of unfavorable hunting conditions? All he can do is make a good faith effort to find elk for his hunters to shoot.

While my Scottish stalking experience involved dining every evening on white linen at a fine country hotel while sporting coat and tie after having bathed following the rigors of the day's stalking, the Idaho experience involved living without running or hot water for a week and shaving and washing only if willing to risk the derision of one's fellows. Bad manners were *de rigueur*: belching, misusing eating utensils, wolfing food, complaining to the cook and introducing unsavory topics during the eating period. It seemed almost a caricature of the stereotyped hunting camp— men intentionally, gleefully shedding their minor social graces.

I witnessed a sharp contrast between the Protestant Ethic in American-style and European hunting. The issues are effort and "productive leisure." The issue of effort is the issue of an oft-encountered American attitude of "no pain, no gain" found in weight-lifters, runners and gymnasts, playing, walking, running through pain. I experienced severe problems with my knees and feet while hunting both Scottish red stag and American elk (wapiti). Although there was the personal pressure to not waste the days of hunting by resting, that attitude was much more rejected in the American elk hunting camp than in the Scottish sporting hotel. The European hunter seems willing to accept only a limited amount of discomfort as the price of his sport. Evidence for this comes from the fact that one of the most common European hunting methods is the hochsitz, or "high seat" or "stand" in which the hunter resides while waiting for the game to appear. Long hours climbing over hills and through valleys is much less common, although not altogether absent, in the

European case. The stand hunting would be typical where prey animals have demonstrated regular habits of movement which can be intercepted by the high seats. Climbing and descending, however, are features of mountain game hunting in Europe for chamois or ibex.

The second issue is "productive leisure." In Europe (Scotland) the search, stalk and shooting are the pleasures derived from this sport. The meat, as discussed earlier, is not owned or retained by the hunter and he shows little or no concern about its preservation and disposal. In the U.S., proper care and utilization of the meat are considered integral parts of the hunters' sporting ethic. One who "wastes" game is dismissed with as much or even more disdain than one who "hogs" shots, does not share in camp chores or handles firearms carelessly.

## A RETURN TO IDAHO FOR SPRING BLACK BEAR HUNTING

My elk hunting in Idaho in the Fall was spectacularly unsuccessful in terms of the standards of productive leisure as defined by either utilitarian or dominionistic hunters (Kellert 1979). I never even saw a bull elk, the object of my quest. The main outcome for me was that many common features of the hunting experience I observed and described. Thus the experience was of great value because of what it demonstrated about the social-psychological processes evoked in an unsuccessful hunting trip as defined by the two most common hunter motivations. (On the other hand, the Idaho wilderness was exquisite in its rugged beauty.)

However, the outfitter convinced me to return in the spring to hunt black bear ($800 for 5 days/travel extra). He claimed that was a much easier form of hunting than pursuit of elk. I purchased a spring hunt, skeptical about the wisdom of trusting the outfitter a second time. What follows is my hunting diary which has been only slightly edited. I will try to isolate the significant features of my experience after the narrative.

SATURDAY, MAY 21

1. Got up at home and took shower, prepared to leave and then noticed it was only 12:59 A.M. Went back to bed until 3 A.M.

2. Left for Indianapolis at 3:40 A.M.

3. Uneventful trip—didn't get sleepy. No problem getting bags on shuttle bus or finding parking space near to shuttle stop. No trouble dragging bags to NorthWest counter.

4. Ate breakfast (pancakes and sausage) in restaurant in airport.

5. Plane to stop in Minneapolis, Great Falls, then Missoula.

6. Plane left Minneapolis 25 minutes late but made up the time somehow!?

7. Got to Missoula on time. Met Jeff, guide for other camp in October. However, my bags and guns did not arrive. Turned out that they had not gotten on the plane in Minneapolis and then were sent to Billings, Mont. which did not go on to Missoula in time.

8. Went to town with guide in Missoula. Ate lunch at McDonald's and went to gunshop/surplus store. Returned to airport and found out that bags were found but not to arrive until 9:38 P.M.

9. So, left for camp, about 6-7 hours away because Hoodo Pass is snowed shut. Direct route takes only about 2 hrs! Drive was beautiful! Always seemed to be driving along a river, creek, streams. High water and fast-flowing over rocks, rapids. Saw mule deer and elk along way. My bags will be picked up by another guide who will go out early on Sunday morning.

10. At camp by 9 p.m. and met other new hunters. Man and wife with son from Streator, Illinois. Wife of son to arrive on Wednesday. She is niece of Rollo, math and computer science professor at my university. Small world!! Hunter from last week, cousin of Dan (guide) shot big bear, over 6 1/2 feet, 8 o'clock on Saturday night, just before we arrived. He was ecstatic. Had borrowed rifle to do it, shot it at about 250-350 yds! Left entire unskinned carcass on hill. Will be retrieved Sunday morning.

SUNDAY, MAY 22

1. Bear retrieved (skin and skull) but no license tag to attach. Therefore, is illegal to display. I took picture of it on table beside cook tent. Left in bag. I worry about hair slipping, but...it's his bear! Temp. in upper 80s to slightly over 90. Sat around drinking Kool-aid and tea, squashing carpenter ants (large black ones) and talking with hunters and guides. Bought Buck ax I had been looking for since Texas in November from newest guide (Vance) for $5 and Buck sheath knife for $10. Great deal for me! He said the ax was too light for the work and the knife was too clumsy. Wonderful!!

2. Went road hunting with Vance in evening since my equipment had not arrived and I did not want to climb a hill with my good shoes on. Along road, up toward the snowed-in pass

saw old cow moose feeding along the road on mountain side, saw a dozen mule deer, several whitetails and 3-4 cow elk feeding on mountainsides.

3. Went with guides to pick up older Streator hunter who was on bear stand on logging road because it had started to rain. Stopped raining, so we (myself and two guides, Vance and Dan) drove to cedar tree grove of ancient vintage. The old cedars averaged 10-15 feet in diameter. Hollow inside—I crawled inside one and shined flashlight up 30 feet of hollow tree.

4. Young hunter from Streator went with Jeff (guide) to 5-mile camp on horses. When they returned, we learned that they had seen a bear at long distance and about 50 elk feeding. Never got close enough to bear to shoot. Bear came out close to elk and neither paid any attention to the other. Returned on horses after dark!

5. *Supper!* Truly memorable. Cook (Lynn) had baked chicken with commercial coating (Shake-n-Bake). Funny taste! New spice?? Turns out she had oiled bake pan with lemon-scented dish soap!! She was mightily embarrassed, but the guides were delighted with her mistake. Occasion for great hilarity!

6. *Fantasies* of bear hunters. Each seems to own and carry a mental image of "his bear," how big, what color. Do other sports have such fantasies about a trophy they hope to achieve? The perfect score, game, reward, trophy??

MONDAY, MAY 23

1. Went in evening to rock face on hillside, overlooking a bait on the opposite side of meadow. Also, carcass of bear shot on Saturday is about 50 yds. away. Quite a climb up and down but not too bad on legs and knees. Came down in semi-darkness. Rode horses across small but deep river. Awful bother to bring horses just so hunter won't get feet wet. But, I appreciated it. Saw nothing at bait. Carcass of bear shot on Saturday may serve as another bait.

2. When returned to camp, found Mike the outfitter had returned and the two Illinois hunters had gotten bears! Dan R. got big (6' 3") black which had teeth worn down, suggesting 15-16 years old. Shot with 270 Win. using 160 gr. Barnes bullet (blew up inside) at about 100 yds. 1-shot! Big head!

3. Dan's stepson, Russel, shot brown black-bear at 5-mile camp at 200-300 yds. while walking, with 7 mm Weatherby Mag. Russel and Jeff left whole carcass to be skinned next morning.

Mother (Anne) said she was glad that both got bears as she hated thought of riding home with them if only one or none had a bear!

TUESDAY, MAY 24

1. Illinois people reassure me that today is my day to kill a bear. I watched them skin the big, old black bear and measure its hide. Negotiated with Mike to buy massive elk antlers ("sheds").

2. 6 p.m. and on same hillside stand with Dan (guide). I lay around all day because I have a cold coming on. Had stomach cramps before I left camp. Climb up hill seemed to resolve them! Dan did fine job of climbing hill in stages. No bear appeared. Lost flashlight as I fell when crossing stream.

WEDNESDAY, MAY 25

1. Rode with Jeff back to 5-mile camp and climbed steep, steep hill and then climbed still farther up into a 15-ft. tree-stand. Bait is only 20 yds. away. I climbed up on steel cleats in tree plus branches. Nylon safety belt to hold me up. Not supposed to move, cough, etc. My cold caused me to cough and mosquitoes caused me to move and hard seat caused me to stretch occasionally. Fifteen minutes after I got up in stand, 2 mule deer (doe and button buck) walked noisily beneath my stand without looking up and seeing me. I was in the stand from 4:30 p.m. to 9 p.m. Wondered if Jeff would return to talk me down out of stand. Heard and saw very little else except for the mule deer. They bolted off after they got downwind from the stand. Did they smell me? Jeff talked me down out of stand with flashlight and verbal directions for feet. Scary to take first step out of stand! Then, walked rather rapidly down the hill in the dark, with flashlight. I backed down in many places and found, once again, that it worked well. Not too hard on knees. Once off the hill, we had a 5-mile, 2-hour ride back to camp in the dark! Jeff instructed me to just trust my horse (Belinda, same horse I rode in October). Moon went behind clouds soon after we started back and then it began to rain! Not hard, but just enough to dampen spirits. Worry about my gun getting wet in saddle scabbard. Got back to camp at 11 P.M. Rifle not too wet! Changed all ammo in elastic cartridge holder for fresh ones as afraid they might have gotten too wet. When returned to camp, found "Moose-Man" visiting again. He had been there the previous night. Introduced to me, by Anne, as

Mike's friend. He is an alcoholic (about 40+ years old) who was thrown out of his parent's house and lives in his car. His name came from the fact he shot a small moose last fall just down from our base camp. He has a crazy laugh and talks in disjointed sentences about unrelated topics. Tries to memorize everyone's name. Kept bumming cigarettes from smokers in camp. Everyone seemed amused by him. On this night, as I walked in, he asked me if he could have some of my beer. I looked around and saw the others had told him that the beer was mine and not theirs to share. I said, "sure, have some of the beer I don't have." I went to bed and he asked me as I walked out of the cook tent if he could have one more beer. I said, no, because it might run out. Others said they were going to bed also, and when he left, they got back up and went to the cook tent and played cards and talked until all hours.

THURSDAY, MAY 26

1. Rode horses to 5-mile Camp with Jeff. He has seen a large black bear come out of timber at edge of steep meadow about 6:30 P.M. on two different evenings, drink at stream, graze a bit on grass in the meadow, and return to the timber. There is a bait in that meadow, but the bear is not visiting it in daylight as far as we know. We are going for that one! Ride is two hours. Pleasant, again! Stop at hill which I climbed yesterday. Jeff climbs hill with mule and two pails of bear bait to replenish the stand where I sat last evening.

2. We rode past 5-Mile Camp and crossed Vanderbilt River below meadow on horse. The current was so strong and caught my boot on up-river side and almost pulled me off the saddle! Stayed on, however!

3. Rode horses up hill a bit. Got off and walked 50 yds to small pine tree and clump of bushes. I got down and cleared a place to sit and also cleared a shooting lane in the direction of where bear had appeared on two of three previous nights. About 4:30. Waited until 6:30 and no bear! Worked hard to avoid coughing too loudly. Jeff above me, sleeping for a while and watching with me.

4. About 8:10-8:15, Jeff whistled quietly at me. I looked up at him and he whispered, "Bear!" and pointed across the meadow about 70-80 yards away. Standing at the edge of the timber was a large black beautiful bear. Stood in stark contrast to the green of the timber and surrounding vegetation. He looked huge to me. I

looked again at Jeff and he grimaced and said in a whisper, "Shoot him!" I had to move my rifle from one side of the the pine tree to the other because the bear was lower on hillside than we expected. I looked at him through the rifle scope and he began moving down hill. My sighting was obscured by a leaf. I got him in the scope again, took off the safety and aimed for his shoulder. Pulled trigger and had no sense of sound or recoil from my .300 Winchester Magnum, Ruger No. 1 single-shot rifle. There was the sound of the bear being hit! A sad sound!! The bear stumbled and began falling immediately, rolling down the meadow hillside. He was stopped by a small bush. Rolled to within 10 feet of the carcass of the bear shot on hillside on Monday by Russel D.

5. Jeff got up immediately and started across the meadow to the bear. I reloaded, shaking a little bit, and got up and moved with him, asking if he wanted the rifle for a follow-up shot? He declined, stopped, walked back and shook my hand and congratulated me! We approached the bear. It didn't move. Jeff kept saying, "This is a big bear!" We took some pictures immediately because the light was fading and we had no flash equipment with us. Jeff asked that I not put my rifle across the bear because that "demeans the animal" (curious belief that I should have explored further). Write to Jeff about it. Or ask Mike.

6. Jeff started to skin the bear with a folding hunting knife (I have one similar). Soon light faded and I started holding the flashlight for him. Also, I held paws in various positions. We (he) started skinning about 8:30-9 P.M. and it took almost two-three hours to complete skinning, taking penis bone, gall bladder, and back-straps (meat) and to pack it up in bundle to put on the mule. Jeff put the hide with paws and head attached in a feed sack. Then Jeff shouldered it and walked down hill ahead of me with light, rifle, back pack. I stumbled a lot and fell over a log once. No walking stick tonight.

7. Brought horses and mule up to bear pelt. Jeff loaded it on. Horses only slightly spooky. Mule fairly calm. (Jeff said smell of bear's blood made them uneasy.) Jeff roped it down on pack saddle and led the mule and his horse (Luke) down to river we had to cross. On the way down the pelt bag was unbalanced and came off. Jeff had to repack it into a longer pack and rope it onto the pack saddle once again. We mounted the horses and Jeff led the mule across the river without mishap. He was afraid the pelt might come off in the rough river crossing. No such bad luck! I urged my horse, Belinda, into river and kept my feet up more than

first time. She stumbled a bit and did fine but crossed over to a point on the opposite side which seemed to have a deep offshore bottom and high banks. She ended up facing upstream and slowly taking steps against the current. Then she seemed to want to get out by going over the high bank next to us! I got ready to bail off if she faltered; but, she put first one front hoof, then second one, up over the bank and heaved us both up, up over the bank, onto dry land! What a relief. The saddle really pitched and heaved, but I held on and stayed on top of it and her! My boots were soaked by the crossing and my feet remained fairly cold during the trip back to camp. I had followed Jeff's advice, I guess, and trusted my horse to make the best moves for both of us! How true it was! This was especially true on the trail at night when the hunter cannot see the trail and its many obstacles! Time now about 11:45-midnight. Jeff said he was concerned about the pelt slipping, so he decided to walk, leading the mule and his horse. He walked the entire five miles back to camp!! Pelt never slipped again. He said it was more comfortable walking and that he did it several times a year! My foot cramped for some reason in my right stirrup. I thought perhaps the water had caused it to stretch. Perhaps I just lurched when crossing the river. On the trip back I was alone with my thoughts about the bear, my joy, sorrow, guilt (only taking backstraps among the meat portions), sorrow about its death and joy about its size (how silly, juvenile, macho, to start making competitive comparisons with other bears shot so far. I had secret delight that mine might be the biggest in camp!) I thought about how that would disappoint Dan R., whose big bear was very impressive to me earlier in the week. How would Mike react? Were they worried about us? Turns out they waited until midnight to eat dinner. It was to be the grand meal of the week— turkey, apple pie, ice cream!

8. We got back at 2 A.M.! Mike got up to greet us, unrolled bear pelt and turned it upside down on skinning table. Jeff and Mike tended to the horses and then we went in and had dinner at 2:30 A.M. Turkey, gravy, pie and ice cream. Got to bed about 4:00 A.M. Had no trouble sleeping and no dreams about the bear.

FRIDAY, MAY 27

1. 8 A.M. Guide, Vance, got me up with a sip of Jack Daniels bourbon. Wanted me down at the skinning table for pictures of hide. I took my rifle even though it was raining! Congratulations offered all around and pictures taken with various combinations of

guides, hunters. Then spent rest of day riding in truck with Mike to town. Went to taxidermist and gave specifications for rug. Went to Mike's house in Orofino. Talked about outfitting as business.

2. Mike plans to grow into new areas and offer quality hunts. Keeps careful records of when and where bears are sighted and shot and predicts when and where they will appear again. Concerned about monitoring and predicting carrying capacities of various gamelands in his areas.

3. He financed purchase of new area by selling packages of five elk hunts for $8000 (normally $2250/hunt). The buyer can resell hunts at whatever price for a profit or merely share the bargain with his friends. The buyer also received five percent of the business in the new area.

4. Mike claimed that he learned to bait bears while working for someone else. Sure knows how to do it [no longer legal in Idaho]. I talked to four hunters on trip home (in airport in Great Falls) who had been hunting in Clearwater National Forest with an outfitter who does not use bait. They only saw one bear, sow with three cubs, and heard a bear in thick cover at 20 yds. which they could not see to shoot. Said the snow had kept big boars in hibernation and only sows with cubs were out yet. Quite a contrast to my experience. When I asked about baiting, they quickly and adamantly answered, "No, the outfitter did not bait." They also said they had been out here last year and the weather had been much warmer during the same week last year.

SATURDAY, May 28

1. Lynn and Dan (the killer) took me to Missoula through Hoodoo Pass which was now open. Dropped me at airport but refused my offer of breakfast as they wanted to go to town and buy some personal and camp supplies. Uneventful trip back to Indianapolis other than worrying that the elk antlers I had purchased would be damaged in transit. Ill-founded fear. They arrived in fine form. Porter at Indianapolis waited with my bags while I got the car. He recounted being in the South Pacific during W.W. II. and shooting wild pigs for natives on various islands. He said they would herd the pigs past the G.I.s who would shoot them with their army rifles. The pigs were tossed on the fires without cleaning, he said, and thus he never was tempted to taste the meat!

What does the diary reveal? Well, it reveals my concerns, the salient concerns of the hunter who worries about things which can go wrong with a hunt: not getting up in time, not finding long-term parking at the airport, not making connecting flights on time. The only thing I did not worry about was my luggage getting lost, which happened! In actual hunts very simple things can disrupt plans and, since most American hunters must save carefully to purchase such adventurous fantasies, the threats of disruptions weigh heavily on hunters' minds.

The diary records early descriptions of new hunting companions, the search for common grounds and a basis for mutual acceptance. Also, notable mishaps are preserved: lost luggage, dinner baked with soap instead of oil, real or imagined illnesses which threaten to prevent the hunter from going afield, etc. A record of the long search for the prey and the comparisons between one's own hunting "luck" and the luck of my companions were duly noted. I tried to infuse the diary with the note of polite patience and good humor about my lack of luck and the good luck of the other hunters. Then, when I am successful, I go on at great length about the various elements which made the success so memorable: the long ride, treacherous river crossing, the fatal shot, the long process of removing the hide, the long trek back to camp, arrival at 2 A.M. and the celebration dinner at three in the morning.

The final day's entry records my attempts to find out more about the purposeful construction of the hunting fantasies being sold by the outfitter. The goal is to develop a hunting experience which is relatively easy physically but not too easy. The baiting of the prey must be handled with finesse because the practice is considered unsporting in some hunting circles, though legal in Idaho at the time of my hunt [no longer legal in Idaho]. The outfitter has the problem of delivering success without overstressing his "resource base," the supply of game animals in his access areas. The cost/benefit ratios of this kind of hunting are much more favorable than with elk hunting. The costs in money and physical effort are much lower and the chances of success are much higher.

### AMERICAN HUNTING, TEXAS STYLE:
### MOVEMENT TOWARD THE EUROPEAN SYSTEM

The next hunting experience of my sabbatical research was obtained in the brush country of south-central Texas. This trip took place because I accepted the generous invitation of a Texas hunter whom I had met in Scotland to join him on his hunting lease for a weekend of hunting. The amount of game I encountered in Texas is only dreamed or read about by most American hunters! More about that soon.

Texas shares some of the traits of the European system of hunting: the state licenses the hunter and the hunter purchases the right to trespass on land not his own in order to pursue game. The game becomes, de facto, the property of the land owner to sell on the hunting market by means of the hunting lease. Leases cost somewhere around $4/acre/year to purchase. Most hunting leases are shared by small groups of hunters who typically minimize the number of shares in order to avoid diluting the hunting experiences provided on the lease.

The other form of access to hunting in Texas is to pay to hunt on the premises of game ranches which are often fenced and stocked with exotic game from other continents. On many of these ranches, the hunter only pays trophy fees for the animals he actually shoots. Two other forms of access are less common. The state maintains some public hunting areas; but, demand for access is so great that a lottery decides who may enter. The second form is found on some hunting leases where the owner sells "day hunts" to hunters for a set trespass fee. On the lease I visited, the previous year's day hunters were permitted to hunt for $75/day. The lease holders negotiated an end to that practice with their lease renewal the year I hunted with them. As a result of this hunting access system, much land that is marginal for other purposes generates some income for its owner in the form of lease fees.

I cannot verify that the features of the hunting lease I visited are typical of all hunting leases; however, the patterns witnessed there are likely to be duplicated elsewhere.

The expenses of equipping the lease with hunting facilities were mainly the responsibility of the lease holders on the lease I visited. The one exception was that the land owner had provided a new 14-foot-wide house trailer for use as a hunting camp. It was equipped with heat, lights, water, etc. The lease holders had planted oats as a feeding supplement for deer and had installed hunting seats and some solar powered feeding stations which regularly dispense small amounts of grain (corn) in order to help hold the game in the area. The lease, approximately 2000+ acres, was shared by five families. It offered a variety of game: whitetail deer, two varieties of quail, wild turkeys, cottontail rabbits, jackrabbits, feral pigs and doves. I have never witnessed such vast numbers of deer and quail! We traveled about the lease by means of a jeep, and a trip in any direction reliably produced sightings of deer and quail. The state-set kill limits testify to the abundance of game animals. A deer hunter may legally take four deer during the season, only two of which may be bucks. The daily limit of quail is 16.

A typical daily routine of hunting: We rose at 5 A.M., planned the day's hunting and traveled to our hunting seats a little after 6 A.M. We remained in the seats until around 9 A.M., then returned to the hunting trailer for breakfast. After an artery-hardening meal of eggs and bacon we departed in the jeep to roam the lease looking for coveys of quail. No dogs were used on this lease. When a covey was spotted from the road, we would walk up to the covey, shooting as the quail flushed and pursuing each covey on foot until it had scattered beyond easy contact. Then we would resume our search by jeep. My host claimed that our day was very poor and that on opening day a different covey was encountered about every 50-100 yards along the track. I thought my day's hunting success was quite good, but I was willing to accept his testimony about what the lease was capable of producing.

In the middle of the afternoon, quail hunting was terminated so that we could return to the trailer, clean the quail already taken and prepare for the evening stand hunting. The evening hunt lasted from about 4 P.M. until dark. At that time all hunters returned to the trailer, prepared and ate dinner and reviewed the day's sightings of game.

The lease holders exhibited a variety of hunting philosophies. For one example, my host was eager to extract a maximum amount of game from the lease. He believed in harvesting "inferior" bucks and many does from the lease each year in the interest of improving the hunting and obtaining the venison which he and his family greatly enjoyed eating. He also believed that the quail population could sustain maximum harvests continually. Other lease holders I met displayed different philosophies. One man was primarily interested in quail hunting and rabbit hunting with his grandsons. He did not want to bother with cleaning a deer. His son was a trophy buck hunter who had not shot a deer in five years while waiting for the chance for a shot at the "big buck." My host complained privately that this hunter was doing the lease no favor by refusing to shoot does and inferior "spike" bucks.

On the last hour of the last day of the hunt, we traveled the perimeter of the lease one last time. On an earlier circuit of the lease, we put up a flock of wild turkeys from a hillside which must have numbered at least 40 birds. What an awesome sight! During this last circuit, my host and I witnessed a group of four small bucks moving along the fence line. I downed an 8-point buck with my host's rifle. We quickly dressed the deer, boned the meat, deposited it in the cooler and headed for home. I had seen no bucks but many does close in during my hunting tours in the shooting towers. Seeing does and bucks bounding over brush in the distance was a thrilling experience, nonetheless.

**HUNTING IN AFRICA: THE ULTIMATE HUNTING FANTASY**
     Big-game hunting in Africa is the ultimate hunting fantasy of many sport hunters. This continent has been characterized throughout the 20th century as displaying the "autumn of the Pleistocene" in terms of the varieties and numbers of free-living wild animals. Most had evolved in the midst of man and had little to fear from indigenous peoples until the advent of gunpowder. When European colonists witnessed the animal fauna, they quickly began the commercial and sporting exploitation of these creatures.
     Explorers, soldiers on leave, gentlemen of leisure, all had representatives who recorded their sporting forays among the animal inhabitants of the "dark" continent. An American President, Theodore Roosevelt, made an early (1909) safari to East Africa after his presidency ended, thus popularizing and legitimizing such sporting campaigns. Famous novelists, such as Ernest Hemingway (*Green Hills of Africa*) and Robert Ruark (*Horn of the Hunter*), continued the popularization of African hunting by their writings in the 1930s and 1950s. Popular films, beginning in the 1940s and continuing in the 1980s have glamorized such hunting. (See chapter 8 for more on this point.) Of course, the sporting press maintains the topic as one of its staples.
     When I planned the research for earlier parts of this chapter, conducted during an academic sabbatical leave, I excluded Africa as too expensive. I could have spent all of the money expended on my six other hunting trips, and more, on a single African hunt. I rationalized the exclusion of Africa by contending to myself that relatively few American hunters ever actually achieve their fantasy; therefore, the types of hunting I could cover were much more typical experiences for contemporary hunters. And any generalizations concerning the meanings of sport hunting in these contexts would be more relevant to a larger segment of the sport hunting population. I was totally surprised, therefore, when I

received a call from a hunter I had met in Scotland who invited me to fill in at the last minute on a budget-priced African hunt in Zimbabwe ($7500/13 days/travel included) It seemed like an opportunity too good to pass up, although I doubted whether I really had the energy to pursue it. Also, the trip commenced 18 days from the date of my learning of it. Usually, African hunting trips are planned years or at least months in advance. To put together the necessary equipment in 18 days was...impossibly crazy! However, I accepted and what follows are my gleanings from that trip.

Sport hunting in Africa is an Anglo-European invention. (See Bartle Bull's definitive treatise [1988] on this topic.) It symbolizes to many the imposition of Western will and values upon African peoples and resources. Those westerners who first invaded the hunting grounds of Africa were explorers who were soon followed by both European and Islamic ivory hunters. Those western ivory hunters who recorded their exploitive deeds often rationalized their acts as providing great quantities of protein for native peoples who lacked the technological means to secure it for themselves.

The early sporting safaris were elaborate expeditions, requiring ground travel by foot, horse or oxcart, with large labor forces to manage the transport and provisioning of the hunting camps. These expeditions often lasted for months and could only be afforded by wealthy persons of leisure. Royalty from many European nations purchased such sporting adventures, which served to further popularize the activity. With the advent of the motor car and motor launch, travel in the interior of Africa became more efficient, less expensive and thus available to sportsmen with smaller purses. Many consider the 1920s and 1930s as the golden age of African sport hunting due to the cost/benefits ratios then present. Even during the 1930s, safaris typically lasted from a month to six weeks or more. Obviously, such expeditions were not for every purse. Hollywood stimulated interest in African hunting by producing several movies containing hunting themes (see chs. 9 and 10 for more details). Also various Hollywood notables bought safaris for themselves.

With the coming of de-colonialization of African states in the 1950s, 1960s and 1970s, the safari business entered a time of turmoil and instability. Some nations (i.e., Kenya) ended sport hunting in the 1960s after deciding to preserve its animals for photographic safaris only. Many nations had their game populations ravaged by unrestrained poaching by those desperate for meat or inflamed with greed for ivory, horns, skins (anything of commercial value). Many nations, however, recognized the power of safari hunting to generate foreign currency exchange and have encouraged its continuance under strict government regulation.

For example, in Zimbabwe, where I hunted, the government recognizes three kinds of sport hunting, two of which are of financial value to the government. The first kind takes place on private land where the hunter is the personal guest of the land owner. As long as the land owner does not charge the hunter, there is no fee collected by the government. However, when such hunting results in trophies, they cannot be removed from the country. The second type takes place on private land where the hunter is paying a fee to the land owner. In this circumstance, the land owner must employ a professional hunter to guide the hunter and charge a government-specified trophy fee for each animal collected. The fee is to be collected in foreign currency which must be exchanged for Zimbabwe dollars immediately. Also, the government charges an export fee for each trophy taken out of the country. A third form of sport hunting takes place on government lands under lease to safari companies. These are the most expensive hunts. The private safari companies may also arrange for hunting on private land according to fees which insures a profit to the land owner as well as to the safari operator.

The hunts just described represent the most typical African safari of the 1980s and 1990s. Lasting from seven days to three weeks or more, they provide the hunter with the opportunity to hunt a variety of game animals associated with Africa at a relatively low cost. The glamour animals of Africa, the "big five" are very expensive, not available many places, and often require the purchase of a longer hunt. The "big five" include lion, elephant, cape buffalo, leopard and rhinoceros. Rhino are virtually extinct in Africa and are the most expensive when available. (Rhino are almost never available because of their almost certain permanent listing as endangered species with C.I.T.E.S.)

Some social psychological images assist in ordering my experiences. At its best, hunting is conducted according to a sporting ethic which specifies in implicit terms the means of fair chase used to pursue game animals, the ways the hunter treats his hunting partners and the demeanor with which the hunter conducts himself in response to success as well as to failure. I witnessed several forms of deviation from the hunting ethic worthy of mention. One form involved hunting at night with spotlights, what is called in the United States "jacklighting." The hunters drive through game areas, hoping to encounter animals who are momentarily immobilized by spotlights shining in their eyes. Their hesitation and well-lighted countenances allow the hunter time to shoot. The owner of the ranch on which I hunted recalled that in his 50 years of hunting big game, 90 percent or more of his game animals had been taken at night by these means. The rationalization is that during daylight hours the human hunter is disadvantaged by the superior senses of the prey species. At night, the human hunter evens the odds with his own enhancement of his senses by technological means: vehicles, spotlights and telescope-sighted rifles. Several of the family members on the ranch expressed their quiet disapproval of night hunting even though they participated in it in order to exploit the commercial possibilities of the game on the ranch.

The sporting code ideally holds regardless of circumstances. One conforms even in the face of the worst luck in encountering prey species. However, African hunting produces temptations to ignore the code. First, the enormous costs in time and money to pursue African game produce what we might term cognitive dissonance. Here I am, having traveled a long, weary way, at great cost, to hunt animals. I consider myself a rational person. Would a rational person come all this way, at this cost and not be intensely concerned about success? Is it rational to observe all the niceties of the sporting code if the cost of such compliance is lack of success? How can I explain my "noble" failures back home? Will such noble conformity to the code compensate me in the long run with pleasant memories of a once-in-a-lifetime hunting trip? Who goes hunting to Africa and comes home with little or nothing? In the face of some combination of these questions, the hunter is likely to be tempted to use less savory methods when the most sporting means fail: spotlight hunting at night, waiting at waterholes during the dry season, baiting carnivorous prey with game meat.

One delicate part of the sporting ethic covers the treatment of fellow hunters in the gamefields. The ideal is that hunting companions fairly divide the hunting opportunities among themselves to insure maximum satisfactions for all involved. "Game hogging" is the ugly practice of taking more than one's fair share of shots. It generates bad feelings and resentments which sour, at least temporarily, the relationships among hunters.

In my view, I was a victim of such an incident in Africa. One of my hunting companions was a much more experienced hunter than I. He was highly skilled at seeing game, preparing to shoot and actually taking the shot. One afternoon he and I were riding on the back of a truck when he spotted a kudu, an animal I had been unable to collect up to that point in the hunt. He had already collected two; but he jumped off the truck, sat down and got off a shot which downed the animal. I was more furious than I have ever been in a hunting situation even though the shot was on his side of the truck and he was more experienced in executing the final stages of a hunt. Part of his eagerness to shoot was prompted by the fact that he thought he had shot at and missed a lion the previous night. Also, he had walked all that morning and had found nothing to shoot at. Thus, his frustration level was very high and the kudu opportunity provided an escape valve. Nevertheless, other members of the hunting party communicated with me their assessment that I should have been at least offered the shot and given the opportunity to turn it down. Because of my anger, later that afternoon, I took a shot at an impala at too long a distance, from too unsteady a rest, and only wounded it. With bitter irony I recognized that I had come full circle and my own frustrations had mislead me into an unsporting act!

Compared to my other hunting experiences perhaps the most astounding, arresting feature of African hunting is the amazing variety of game offered the hunter. I collected five varieties of African game during my economy hunt: impala, eland, warthog, wildebeast and kudu. Others were offered to me but I declined for various reasons, mostly cost: zebra, sable, giraffe (does anyone seriously consider a giraffe a desirable hunting trophy?), lion, bushbuck, duiker, waterbuck, gemsbuck, hartebeast, elephant. Even the lowest-priced safaris commonly offer ten or more species. Thus, unlike North American or European hunting, where one typically pursues a single species or three at most, the variety available is apparently part of the appeal as well as the aesthetic value of the trophy heads.

The African safari of today is subject to many pitfalls for the aspiring hunter. The rigors and complications of travel, the difficulty in anticipating all expenses involved before hand, the probabilities of engaging honest or dishonest outfitters, all are salient challenges for those who go.

A final note regarding the "fair chase" ethic: I hunted on a cattle ranch of 45,000 acres. The hunting method involved traveling from section to section, seeking information on game sightings by the stock handlers. Other times, long walks in search of game was the tactic selected. The game meat was used by the ranch family, served to hunters, shared with native Africans and dried into a favorite Afrikans' delicacy, "biltong." All three hunter motivations were easily satiated. One did not have to choose among them. The memory of butterflied, Impala tenderloin steaks roasted for breakfast over an open fire will never be lost from the utilitarian portion of my hunter's soul. The massive, yet gracefully spiraling kudu horns on my wall, along with my red deer "royal" stag from Scotland, share equal pedestals of honor on my dominionistic altar. The African landscape in this low-veldt region showed shambled evidences of human habitations from the "basement of time." The animals, the terrain, the lovely people, all could have done no more to kindle the resolve to return in the breast of the naturalistic hunter.

## HUNTING ON A COMMERCIAL GAME RANCH:
## THE FANTASY AND THE FACTS!

Among forms of hunting available to contemporary sportspersons, the last one I wanted to investigate is hunting offered by commercial game ranches. These ranches sell hunters the opportunities to "hunt" and shoot game imported from virtually any point on the globe. These ranches have identified what species from around the world are susceptible to transplantation and survival in U.S. hunting habitats. Asia (India), Africa and Europe have species which can be captured, transported and released on these ranches. The ranches are enclosed but typically include large acreage so that it suggests at least the illusion of free-roaming animals.

Many of the animals offered by game ranches are labeled "exotics," and separate records of these trophies have been established with the encouragement of the industry. This separate record-keeping is necessary because the flagship of record-keeping organizations, the Boone and Crockett Club, enforces strict standards of fair chase which must be documented when an animal trophy is submitted for judging. Among the standards is the requirement that the animal pursued could not have been restrained in any way in its opportunities to escape (such as a fence on a game ranch).

The site of my game ranch research visit is located in the foothills of the Missouri Ozarks. It contains roughly 1000 acres surrounded by a seven-mile-long gameproof fence, and offers visiting hunters either free camping facilities or rooms and meals in a lodge constructed from two double-wide trailer units. The lodge is decorated with mounted heads of game, all of which supposedly were harvested on the ranch. The lodge offers bedrooms for up to eight hunters and video equipment for viewing hunting videos which advertise other hunting opportunities available on this ranch. An artificial lake just below the lodge provides fishing for guests.

The 1000 acres offer open fields, rocky hills and gullies as the terrain in which to seek the ranch's trophies. A manager's trailer, barn for skinning, butchering and temporary cold-storage of carcasses and stock pens for restraining newly arrived "trophy" animals complete the ranch's furnishings.

The lodge offers a video showing the ranch owner explaining what the ranch offers the hunter. The video's opening scenes of the ranch suggest a vast abundance of animals at all times. The owner is interviewed on camera and he states that the majority of the animals are raised on the ranch and that only occasional "infusions" or "injections" of fresh, superior, genetic materials are introduced into the herds. As he puts it, "The state of Missouri manages the indigenous game animals for quantity; we here on the ranch manage for quality."

The owner contends that modern-day hunting in the wilds is so costly in time and money and the success rates are relatively low, especially in something like elk hunting (7-17 percent). The ranch offers a hunter the specific animals s/he wants to pursue, when s/he has the time to pursue them. The hunter pays for only what is shot. The guide and lodging/meals fees are relatively modest. The trophy fees (price of the animals) are substantial but less than the cost of wilderness hunting trips with their marginal expectations of success.

The impression projected is that the choice of a game ranch setting in which to hunt is a rational decision which reduces costs in time and energy while providing a substantial portion of the physical and emotional challenges and rewards provided by a wilderness hunting trip. Other ranches, especially in Texas, stress how they play an important role in preservation and propagation of certain species. Collectively, these ranches may validly claim that they house the largest known populations of X, Y or Z species in the world. Some have reported that they have helped reestablish certain species to their native habitats when original stocks have been depleted by disease, poaching or the various pressures exerted on animal species by growing human populations.

The ranch owner, as an official scorer for S.C.I (Safari Club International) records, conveys the impression that the ranch offers a good chance for harvesting a "record" animal. In short, the impression given is that everyone wins: the animals as threatened species, the sportsperson as a busy but enthusiastic partisan of the hunt and the opportunity to be acknowledged publicly for harvesting record-sized animals.

My discipline teaches that "reality" is a socially negotiated phenomenon subject to controversy, contention, change and possibly only partial consensus. The "reality" of sport hunting is multi-faceted, with many audiences: the hunter himself/herself, fellow hunters, non-hunting sympathizers, non-hunting opponents, operators of hunting experience businesses, to name only the more obvious ones. Each audience group reacts to particular hunting activities separately. The phenomenon of game ranch hunting is probably the least-honored form for many segments of these audiences. The illusions constructed about game ranch hunting are outlined above and are designed to convince potential customers that this kind of hunting is a legitimate alternative open to anyone with the cash. I observed first-hand and heard second-hand some data which would belie the illusions for many segments of the audiences.

First, on the ranch I observed, most of the game present was very tame because of having been fed and because of constant exposure to humans. How could any sportsperson justify shooting a bison or elk, both of which could be approached by vehicle to within ten feet? Also, at least on this ranch, most of the animals advertised for sale were not present at all times, being allowed to reproduce with occasional assistance from outside genetic sources, as was suggested by the owner in the promotional video mentioned above. Perhaps I was visiting and observing during the season when the stock was especially low, (preparing for winter?) but I learned that the ranch had received shipments of several kinds of animals in the week preceding my visit. Specifically, they had taken delivery of a shipment of nine trophy-sized whitetail bucks and six Russian boars. I assume these had been released to roam within the 1000-acre confines of the ranch.

In general, the price for harvesting of animals is substantial, from $400 for a razor-back hog to $10,000-$20,000 for a white rhino. Herein lies a dilemma. The ranches often advertise: "You only pay for what you kill." However most of the more expensive animals are only purchased by the ranch and shipped in shortly before the hunter is scheduled to arrive. I assume the ranch must pay for the animals when they are removed from the premises of the ranch which imported or raised them. If the hunter shoots and wounds an animal, he must pay for it whether or not it is recovered. But, if the hunter does not shoot an animal purchased for him, then what are the financial arrangements? Can the animal be returned for a refund?

A small group of javelinas (wild pigs from our southern border states) was penned near the skinning/butchering barn. These javelinas had been imported to this ranch because two hunters wanted to harvest one each. My guide told me on the day before the hunters' arrival to "hunt" them that the javelinas were so mean and dangerous they would not be released on the ranch. The hunters would have to shoot them in the pen. (A father-son pair from Laredo, Texas, visiting the ranch said javelinas in Texas were numerous and fairly benign.) However, the hunters were told that if the pigs were released and they got away, the hunters would have to pay anyway. One of the hunters had just returned from a very successful hunt in British Columbia where he used fair-chase methods to secure his trophies: moose, caribou, mountain goat, mountain sheep, wolverine. But he shot his javelina in the pen. What did he think about this? (It cost him $500 to poke a gun through a fence and dispatch his pig. Why so expensive if so numerous in Texas?) I saw the one hunter just returned from British Columbia shortly after he killed his javelina. I may have imagined it, but he seemed a bit sheepish. As the animal was being skinned, he pointed out to me the teeth and made a comment about the damage they could do. That comment suggested that he was really saying to me, "You don't know how I shot this javelina, but these teeth explain why I had to shoot it in the pen." He never mentioned the circumstances of the kill.

My own hunting experience involved pursuit of a Russian boar. This was almost the least expensive animal ($500) and the one with the best reputation as food. My guide convinced me that a Russian sow would be better eating. We drove around the periphery of what was called the "hog lot." 'This was a 40-50 acre subdivision of the ranch which was fenced off from the rest in order to try and control the movements of the razor-back and Russian pigs. The explanation was that the pigs do too much damage when allowed to roam freely. Not seeing any animals from the truck, we started walking. I could have shot a Russian boar within 50 yards of the truck. The guide asked if I wanted to take it. I decided to hunt on and we walked several hours, coming upon but losing two or three other hogs before I came upon a Russian sow which I shot at about 70 yards. My wife was present and seemed impressed with the shot. Her appreciation was gratifying, although the shot was taken from a rest against a tree. My hunting completed, I helped the guide drag the Russian sow up the hill to the road where we loaded it onto the back of his truck and carried it off to the skinning/butchering pole. I mentioned above that we had not seen any animals close enough to shoot during our walk in the woods. However, around the butchering post, there were now several Russian pigs trotting about, eating venison scraps from the butchering of several deer the previous day. Any sense of accomplishment I might have felt by finally felling a Russian hog evaporated when we had to shoo them away from the skinning station.

One hunter claimed he came to the ranch several times a year and hunted whatever he could because he loved to hunt. On his first night at the ranch, he took a fallow deer by spotlighting from a truck and then spent over an hour poring over the record book to discover how his might place. Apparently the jacklighting method does not invalidate the record in the "exotics" category. This hunter also claimed that he has his name in the SCI record book four times from game ranch exotic heads.

The owner claimed that the ranch was so big that people could get lost. Therefore, every hunter had to hunt with a guide. I believe the guide also serves more like a solicitous clerk in a department store who hovers near the customer to keep track of what is being purchased and to encourage the "shopper" to take a more expensive commodity to the cash register.

## DISCUSSION

Objectively, the meaning of hunting is very subjective. Just as a child who can imagine a campfire on the tile floor of a classroom or a cave in a closet or a fighter airplane from an overturned kitchen chair, the hunter can erect his own fantasy about the meaning of the killing pursuit he purchases.

Various rationalizations can be developed by the hunters and/or promoted by the operators of the game ranches.

a. The owner on his video described the ranch as a place where animals from around the world could be hunted safely without risk of traveling to dangerous parts of the globe and at lower cost and less time.

b. Numerous hunters often choose to use exotic weapons which increase the chances of the animals escaping: pistols, bows, black powder rifles or shotguns.

c. One visitor to the ranch was a father (one from Laredo) who was taking his 14-year-old son hunting for the experience of practicing shooting and hunting to test the depth of the son's enthusiasm as well as to promote "togetherness." This son had demonstrated his enthusiasm in two ways. First, he saw the ad in a hunting magazine and called and made all the arrangements for the trip. The second way the son demonstrated his enthusiasm is that he shot a sitka deer ($1000-$1500) and two blackbucks ($2000-$2500 per animal). The son had already killed 14 whitetail deer in his brief hunting career.

d. My rationalization, in addition to this research, is to try out various hunting firearms which I will never live long enough to use in normal circumstances.

Superficially, these commercial game ranches share features with hunting in Europe. Game in Europe is often raised especially for the hunting season as is the case of pheasants all over the British Isles and many locations on the Continent. Game parks of vast acreage contain carefully guarded herds of red deer, roe deer, wild boars, which are open to hunters who can pay the considerable trophy fees. The animals in the European case can be considered to be "free-roaming" in all of the habitats which remain unpopulated by homo sapiens. In the United States, our game ranches contrast dramatically with the vast public lands still open to hunters. Thus, there is as yet no tradition of defining as sporting the hunting of animals especially provided for the hunt (and perhaps never will be, depending on the outcome of the political battles over retaining hunting of animals as an accepted activity of citizens). The American case, as sampled in my research site visit, is rather crass and direct in its means of providing/guaranteeing game for the hunter. A more subtle construction of the illusion of fair chase would greatly enhance the game ranch experience in the U.S. This must be accomplished if it is to survive and appeal to a wider audience of American hunters.

# Chapter Seven

# Trophy Seeking as Sports' Immortality in Hunting and Fishing

The trophy hunters are the elite thrill-seekers of the shooting world, the so-called "killing conservationists." The dedicated searchers for high-calibre action with rifle, bow or camera through the most majestic game fields of the world. Be they taxi drivers..., factory workers..., company executives..., or industrial czars..., these selective hunters share a common love of the great outdoors, and an understanding of and feeling for their quarry, which non-hunters find paradoxical. They hunt the giant males of the animal kingdom—old warriors past their prime living on borrowed time, trophy animals which have reached an advanced age by eluding hosts of Nimrods....
(Allison)

...Trophy hunting has to be one of the lowest, basest, meanest characteristics of man. Killing may be necessary at times, but it is never pretty or honorable. (*Time* EB6)

## INTRODUCTION

Hunting is a controversial "sport" in modern societies. Once required of us all, it now is preserved among elites and significant minorities of working- and middle-class males in industrial societies. Attempts to defend the practice of seeking and ending the lives of fellow life forms rely on assertions of food value, recreational values in out-of-doors activities, and management ("pruning") functions of conducting sustainable harvests of game birds and animals (whatever species have the misfortune of being of interest to hunters).

One variety of hunting, both of animals and fishes, does not seek food, outdoor recreation or the role of harvester of nature's surplus. This variety seeks trophies of the hunt that are preserved and, often, displayed as relics of past quests and conquests. What is trophy hunting? Why do humans engage in it? What are its meanings for its practitioners? These questions will be addressed in the following pages. The general theme is another examination of humans' attempts to devise meaningful games for themselves which serve various psychological, social-psychological and group status needs. It also addresses, by this example, how humans justify, rationalize, neutralize objections to practices which are voiced by significant others in the social environment.

## WHY DO MEN HUNT FOR TROPHIES?

Trophy hunting is as old as hunting as a leisure activity. Relics of past civilizations reveal that mementos of animals killed in the chase were revered and preserved either as display items (bear skulls, deer and elk antlers) or as raw materials for useful objects (knife handles, powder flasks). Whether for display or for religious purposes, these relics seemingly occupied a salient psychological spot in the lives of elites.

Trophies can mean various things to various people. A sample of possible meanings follows:

1. Trophies are mere mementos of a pleasurable activity. They may be merely mental reminders, nothing else.

2. Trophies may symbolize mastery over dangerous forces of nature which may threaten humans (bears, wolves, whales, elephants, lions, tigers). They may testify that the trophy bearer has triumphed in the face of adversity which all who view the trophy can imagine.

3. Trophies can take various material forms, with various meanings:

a. Often the largest of a species is pursued and evidence of its size is preserved (tusks, horns, antlers, skin, skull, etc.) The largest may be the oldest members of an animal community and considered expendable because their reproductive contributions to the species will have dwindled or ended. The largest is often considered the wisest and, therefore, the most difficult to capture. Size comes gradually through surviving successive seasons of the rigors of nature and of other hunters seeking the prey. When the largest is brought down, the hunter has demonstrated his skills in the use of hunting technology and his understanding of animal ways.

b. Trophies may be sheer numbers taken from a prolific game species. This kind of trophy was preserved as "bag" records in game books maintained by hunters of the past. Such records symbolized the skills of the hunter in the use of the tools of the hunt. This kind of hunting fell out of favor at the turn of the century as public consciousness came to consider wild animals as dwindling natural resources.

c. Trophies may consist of the variations of a species or the combination of species which are captured and immortalized in various kinds of "mounts." Possessing specimens of the "big five" of Africa is status-conferring to a hunter among hunting groups. Having specimens from the various deer, elk, moose, bear, mountain and desert goats and sheep is another type of trophy collection. These collections inspire admiration because they represent dedication to a goal, great expense, world-wide travels and experiences and demonstrated skills and knowledge.

4. Trophy hunting may be considered an "art form" (Atamian) in which the hunter/artist creates an artistic experience by managing his medium and tools (the environment, vagaries of weather, skills in use of instruments of the hunt) to pursue a prey. The hunt is a kind of mental, living canvas whose end products reside in the hunter's memory and trophy room.

5. Trophy hunting may produce records which are preserved by organizations who regulate, evaluate and publicize outstanding animals captured by hunters around the world. These organizations have established measurement procedures for evaluation of the merits of the trophies as well as behavioral standards to be observed during the chase. Evidence must be submitted to document that the trophy was taken according to standards of fair chase before the trophy is eligible to be included in the record books. Various organizations in the English-speaking world conduct such recording-keeping programs—Roland Ward, Boone and Crockett Club, Safari Club International, Pope and Young, International Game Fishing Association. Their counterparts exist in other parts of the industrialized world. Periodically, these organizations hold conventions where trophies are displayed, compared and judged.

6. Trophy hunting, along with Olympic medal seekers and other sports records aspirants, may be manifesting a concern with "post-self" evaluations of significant others (Schmitt and Leonard). A kind of immortality can be earned if one enters the sports records books. To be remembered as being the fastest, most

consistent, strongest, most durable or capturing the biggest and/or most variety of game animals/fishes is a goal which motivates countless numbers of sportspersons.

7. Trophy hunters promote the image of themselves as the "killing conservationists": those who live with the paradox of working to preserve what they most love and love to pursue in order to kill and then display as trophies. The organizations sanctioning trophy hunting must contend with the fact that while 70-80 percent of the American public tolerates sport hunting for meat, less than 20 percent is willing to endorse sport hunting as a means of securing trophies (Kellert, "Attitudes"). Trophy hunters seek good public relations by advertising the amounts spent on trophy hunting which support efforts to defend and restore habitat, pay wardens to enforce game laws, and provide foreign exchange for countries which offer trophy hunting opportunities.

## PERSONAL REACTIONS TO TAKING A TROPHY

As part of my investigations into the meanings sport hunting holds for its participants, I spent an academic sabbatical leave participating in various forms of sport hunting available to American hunters. (See ch. 6.) One experience involved red deer stag hunting in Scotland, a sport popularized by Queen Victoria's consort, Prince Albert. On the fourth day of my hunting week I was led into the presence of a trophy-sized stag and allowed to shoot it. (This experience is described in more undisciplined detail in ch. 6.) This, in itself, was a rare trophy in that the largest stags are seldom shot in Scotland because they are expected to contribute their physical traits to succeeding generations through breeding. Through a combination of luck and apparently having convinced my professional stalker that I was worthy of taking such a trophy, I was led through the stalk. I performed in a way I considered admirable in that I placed all of my thoughts and actions at the disposal of the stalker and obeyed his directions precisely. In addition, I was able to overcome an equipment malfunction at the last moment and complete the hunting act by killing the stag with one shot.

My immediate reactions to taking what the stalker called "a trophy of a lifetime" were restrained. I was assaulted by crosscurrents of emotions and thoughts: Why was I allowed to shoot such a magnificent beast? How could I adequately reward the stalker for leading me to such an animal? What should be my demeanor as one who wants to be thought of as a "good sport?"

How could I show proper respect for the fallen stag? These reactions were further stimulated by the head stalker claiming, with a twinkle in his eye, "Yes, that is a real moving van beast!" When I asked what he meant, he replied, "Well, after a gamekeeper allows a beast like that to be shot, the moving van soon appears at his door."

My real reactions to my trophy came in the early morning hours of the next day. I awoke at 2 A.M. and was unable to sleep again for two hours as I tried to record my feelings. I experienced an almost religious-like ecstasy! This beautiful creature had become my responsibility to honor and display in a fitting manner. I did not feel worthy of it, but felt it was an undeserved gift from providence. I felt it was undeserved because I had not exercised any great level of skill in its taking. I was drowned in luck in crossing its path when I did. I truly felt I understood what is meant by "a gift of grace," a gift undeserved, unearned and, therefore, never repayable.

What is a trophy worth? What makes it valuable? Its rarity? The feelings it evokes in the hunter? The joy and gratitude that it has elevated the hunter in stature in the eyes of the hunting fraternity? The religious feelings that the trophy as an undeserved gift of luck and only a slight testimony to skill? I was awed by my felt responsibility for preserving the stored value and magnificence of its physical beauty. I could anticipate the joy it would bring me whenever I look upon it in the future. The head now belongs to me—*or do I belong to it*? I had the strange sensation that I had been assigned the duty of the caretaking of a monument to the sport of red deer stalking in Scotland. The taking of the stag was a peak experience in my life; I had become part of the ages of sportsmen who pursue the red stag and win.

I felt both joy and sadness as I left the hill after causing his death. How could the magnificence of his life be preserved and shared after his death? Taxidermy cannot bring him back to life. His head is but a one-dimensional physical remnant of the meaning of his existence. However, like the Roman Wall in Britain, his head evokes past glories.

Again, this was a total experience—like unlocking a door, lock after lock—preparation, bad luck, behavior according to the code, acceptance by stalker of my worthiness to accept the opportunity to try the stalk; behavior afterward—no "I feel great" or "Look at what I have done," but calm, sober expressions of awe at what had transpired, doubts of worthiness, seeking reassurances that I had not done something selfish by removing this stag from the hill—his progeny would possess the potential for the visual magnificence of their sire. At the time of this writing, the recollection of the death of the royal stag at my hand once again unleashes the flood of emotion that drenched me in its wake.

## FINDING AND MAKING TROPHIES

The trophy hunter is continuously challenged to locate the large, mature males of the prey species which display the spectacular traits making them a trophy. This quest often takes such discriminating hunters to the ends of the earth where these large, fully developed members of their species can yet be found. Such quests are almost always very costly in time and money. Of course, part of the meaning of a trophy can be distilled from the effort invested in finding it. Great expenditures of time and resources may only enhance the meaning with which the trophy rewards its eventual owner. (For a discussion of the temptations to take shortcuts while seeking trophies, see Barness 48-49.) On the other hand, our industrialized, rationalized society imposes the disciplines of prediction, calculation and control over one's time. Outcomes are important to forecast. When a person, successful in this world, retreats from it to pursue an animal trophy, the unpredictable time required may either sooth him with the "contrast value" it offers or provoke his impatience because of the time limits he faces.

What response is possible to those who seek the extraordinary by the clock? In some prey species trophies can be "grown" in various ways. Game ranches, for instance, can control habitat, nutrition and predation threats surrounding their wild inhabitants. Wildlife biology continues to increase its knowledge of the factors which contribute to the trophy qualities of prey species. This knowledge can be and is applied in the production of superior animals. I witnessed this process and its philosophy first hand in Scotland, among the red deer forests, and on the hunting leases and game ranches of Texas (see chapter 6). There these managed animals can be offered to hunters with time constraints in circumstances that still require substantial physical efforts but which offer the certainty that the trophy animals are known to be out there. Many of the established trophy-registering organizations will not recognize trophies taken from game ranches with fences and other obstacles to the free-ranging of their commodity species. In response, the game ranching businesses have organized their own trophy recognition organization which assists in legitimizing the hunting experiences they market.

## CONCLUSIONS

Whatever the future of sport hunting in the world, trophy hunting will be the last to expire because of the willingness of men with money to purchase access to the rare and beautiful members of many species. Thus, the least favored motivation for hunting is most likely to survive, however diminished the opportunities and inflated the costs.

# Part 4

## HUNTING AND FISHING
## AND POPULAR CULTURE

The final chapters introduce the possibilities for tracking the blood sports through the alleys and back streets of popular culture. Books, movies and instructional videos are popular cultural media which project images of these activities as reflected back from the ethers of the surrounding cultural milieu. Chapters 8 and 9 explore and expose how the presentation of hunting and fishing in the mass media of films and popular boys' literature both influence and reflect public attitudes and perceptions of these sports and their traditions. Chapter 10 aims the historical microscope at the process of the commodification of hunting and fishing over the past 150 years.

**Chapter Eight**                    **Portrayals of Sport Hunting in Popular Films[1]**

## INTRODUCTION

In our pluralistic society the hue and cry for the last generation has been for understanding and tolerance of those whose viewpoints, behaviors and values differ from our own. Improving human relations is the goal which has substantially motivated the formation of the United Nations, the creation of departments of sociology, psychology, anthropology and, recently, in a state university system (Illinois), mandated the explicit inclusion of courses which provide "multi-cultural" education for university students.

Attempts by members of political, social or cultural majorities to describe and explain the world views of various minorities are increasingly discounted as being, at best, accurate representations of the stereotypes of minorities held by majorities. The current cant is that women, not men, can best render the viewpoint of women; blacks, not whites, can best render the viewpoints of blacks; homosexuals, not heterosexuals, can best render the viewpoints of homosexuals. Let the group speak for itself through its most articulate, sympathetic members.

### STEREOTYPES OF HUNTERS AND HUNTING

I suspect that sport hunting as a recreation has been portrayed in films most frequently by film-makers who were unsympathetic and/or unacquainted with its values, traditions and rewards. Although possibly not intentional in many cases, the ways in which sport hunting have been portrayed on film have frequently reinforced many negative stereotypes typically accepted by non-hunters and anti-hunters.

A substantial proportion of the films which include a hunting theme portray the hunter as an obsessive, unstable, dangerous, anti-social creature who, at worst, comes to some bad end or causes great harm to other humans as well as the animals he pursues. At best, the hunter in film reforms of his "hunting ways" through some insightful experience. (Exceptions exist to this generalization and will be noted.)

**117**

These films also nurture the stereotype that hunting threatens many species with extinction, encourages violence against nature and promotes "speciesism" (the belief that only the human species has the inalienable right to live but, in turn, has the right to dominate all other species for recreation or profit).

Although I have no direct evidence of the attitudes of film makers dealing with hunting themes, their portraits of hunters suggest definite biases against hunting. Before I examine specific films, let me suggest how hunters define themselves. Their self-images as hunters will provide specific contrasts with how they are stereotyped in popular films.

## THE SELF-IMAGE OF HUNTERS

Any attempt to distill the ways in which hunters view themselves is a perilous undertaking. However, I contend that the following composite description is a reasonable facsimile of how hunters view their sport.

Hunting is a sport of ancient origins which is preserved in our cultural inventory as an archetype of humankind's encounter with nature. The hunter acknowledges that his/her sport is constrained by rules of the chase, is ennobled by the rituals honoring the prey which fall to the hunters' weapons and is misunderstood by significant portions of non-hunters. The hunter sees himself as a consumptive user of a renewable resource. His license fees and excise taxes paid with the purchase of sporting equipment are major sources of the funds which employ state game managers and wildlife law enforcers. Those funds also pay for the defense, preservation and restoration of wildlife habitats without which many game and nongame species could not survive in appreciable numbers. Thus, the hunter believes he is acting responsibly in ways which benefit the nonconsumptive users of wildlife as well. The sport hunter condemns without reservation members of his subculture who defile the sport with various and sundry abuses of its laws, traditions and rituals. He ardently supports stringent penalties for violators of game laws. All the while, however, he remains puzzled and discouraged by those who not only choose not to hunt but also try to stop others from doing so.

## DIMENSIONS OF ANALYSIS

The films will be discussed in terms of the role that hunting plays in the plot and the implied/portrayed character of the hunters. These films portray various types of hunting: sport hunting, commercial hunting (animal trapping, hide hunting) and animal "control" or humans hunting animals as nuisances/menaces to human activities. The non-sporting types of hunting are included because of the attitudes they convey regarding the more basic dispute over the legitimacy of humans taking away animal lives.

The list of films discussed cannot be called inclusive of all of the hunting genre; however, I claim to have found a sizeable proportion of all those that have been available to American audiences. The films will be grouped and discussed in three categories: films portraying pro-hunting themes, films portraying ambivalent themes, and films portraying anti-hunting themes.

## PRO-HUNTING FILMS

The first group of films examined projects a positive image of hunting. Whether the hunting theme is a minor theme or the central theme, these films do not suggest that hunters are dangerous, immoral, or misguided in their choice of recreations. The films frequently suggest that hunting activities are character-building in various ways.

1. *Life of a Bengal Lancer* (1935) shows British military life in India during the early part of this century. The hunting scenes portray the sport of chasing wild pigs on horseback and spearing them with the lances used as a primary weapon of the regiment. This sport was designed to provide practice of a martial skill and opportunities to experience the thrills of the chase. The impressions conveyed are:

a. Hunting of this form provides both practice and entertainment.

b. Skill at this sport conveys status on its practitioners.

2. *Charge of the Light Brigade* (1936) brings to the screen a drama based on Tennyson's famous poem about the Crimean War. British army life for gentlemen officers typically included sport hunting forays against whatever local fauna presented a challenge. The hero of the film saves his royal host during a leopard hunting trip by shooting a charging, wounded leopard. (Given that royal personage's later misdeeds, we should have cheered on the leopard!) This film features hunting in a very minor role in the overall story. The impression presented, however is: Hunting skills are the mark of a gentleman and enable him to act with coolheadedness in times of crisis.

3. *The Bisquit Eater* (1940) tells the tale of two young lads who rescue a runt from a litter of bird-hunting dogs and attempt to make it into a champion bird dog. The impressions conveyed are:

a. Bird hunting is a normal activity of wealthy persons who devote many resources to pursue the sport.

b. A skilled bird dog is a joy to observe in action, even as the action involves pursuing and participating in the death of attractive birds.

c. No apologies are offered regarding the hunting activity.

4. *Sergeant York* (1941) portrays a skilled hunter from the mountains of Tennessee who becomes a military hero in World War I due to the successful use of his hunting skills. The impression conveyed is:

a. Hunting skills are useful in times of war.

b. Skilled hunters can be attractive persons in other ways.

5. *The Macomber Affair* (1947) portrays African safari hunting in a very sympathetic light. The white hunter hero is observant of the hunting regulations and highly committed to the traditions of fair chase in African hunting. The client is portrayed as inexperienced but eager to do things correctly. After a lapse of courage, the client re-establishes his self-confidence and earns the respect of the white hunter. The exhilaration of the hunting experience is fairly portrayed by the client. This film conveys the impressions that:

a. Sport hunting has honorable traditions which ennoble those who observe them.

b. Hunters of good character can be made even better by participation in fair chase hunting.

c. This form of hunting tends to be a sport only the rich can enjoy.

6. *Snows of Kilimanjaro* (1952) includes hunting as one of the pastimes of the author hero of the story. Hunting in Africa by the hero results in a careless accident which produces a life-threatening infection. Hunting is portrayed as a thrilling, satisfying activity. The white hunter guiding the hero is portrayed as a fatherly, wise, professional with sterling character. The portrait of sport hunting projected in the film:

a. Hunting is an exciting sport which provides other satisfactions besides bagging trophies.

b. The wilderness is dangerous and even the most innocent mistake can threaten life.

c. Hunting for sport is pursued by the rich and famous who are bored with other entertainments.

7. *Harry Black and the Tiger* (1958) presents the hero as a noble character who usually acts honorably, even when such actions cause him personal distress. He is a professional hunter who rids human populations of man-eating tigers. The tiger is presented as a malevolent threat to innocent humans. The hero loses his courage temporarily while encountering a tiger but regains it in a final encounter. He shows no remorse about hunting but ends the film with new plans to hunt additional maneaters. The images of hunting portrayed by the film are:

a. Hunting dangerous animals requires courage as well as skill.

b. Carelessness can be deadly in the hunting field.

c. Hunting dangerous animals can be an honorable test of manhood.

d. Some of the most admirable human traits are displayed by those attracted to hunting.

e. Animals which threaten humans become outlaws deserving destruction.

8. *Tom Jones* (1963) includes an old English deer hunt in which dogs pursue the deer; hunters pursue the dogs on horseback and then dispatch the deer when it finally stops from exhaustion after being pursued by both. The hunting sequence was consistent with other scenes of excess in pursuit of pleasure: eating, drinking and copulation. The hunting sequence is lengthy and conveys the following impressions:

a. Hunting inflames the passions, venatical and sexual.

b. A "blood lust" is temporarily evoked in hunters.

c. A grand time is had by all who participate (except the deer).

d. Those most committed to hunting can allow the sport to run their lives.

9. *Zulu* (1964) included hunting as a minor theme in the early periods of the movie. The callow English officer, with no actual military experience, pursued hunting whenever he could in the hills around his military post. The impressions portrayed are:

a. Hunting is a sport of gentlemen officers (historically correct).

b. Hunting skills can prepare a person for courage under combat conditions.

10. *Deliverance* (1972) includes a main character who is fiercely devoted to archery hunting. He epitomizes the machismo commonly associated with hunting: wilderness is the enemy to be conquered; wilderness contains dangerous forces. The impressions projected of hunters are:

    a. Hunting appeals to persons who are unhappy with the values and alleged virtues of civilization.

    b. Hunting provides the ultimate test of one's masculinity.

11. *Zulu Dawn* (1979) has English gentlemen hunters specially selected as military scouts for the regular army during the Matabele wars in Africa. The impression conveyed is that hunting prowess has many military applications.

12. *Death Hunt* (1981) displays no actual hunting but has its main character, a mysterious trapper, using his woodcraft skills to elude pursuers. The prey is a sympathetic character because of the circumstances which caused his pursuit. The impression conveyed is that woodcraft skills useful in hunting can be useful in survival in the wilderness.

13. *Cold River* (1982) pictures an Adirondack guide taking his children on a canoe trip in the wilderness because he fears it is going to be changed forever in the near future (circa 1924). On the trip his son successfully hunts rabbits with a .22 rifle. Fish are caught and cleaned. Later a deer is killed by the boy. The impressions conveyed are:

    a. Hunting is a natural part of life in the wilderness.

    b. Learning to hunt is a useful part of the training of a youth who will live in and near the wilderness.

    c. The main dangers in the wilderness are other humans and failing to respect its natural forces (wild rivers).

    d. Enjoying the wilderness includes hunting as a valid part of the total experience.

14. *Out of Africa* (1985) has one of its main characters as an ivory hunter and safari guide. Hunting is also portrayed in the earliest scenes as a sport of the upper classes. The African hunting scenes convey some of the danger and excitement of such pastimes. The impressions conveyed are:

    a. Hunting can be noble, clean and one of life's peak experiences.

    b. Hunters can be attractive characters, multidimensional, with hunting as an integral part of their identities.

15. *The Shooting Party* (1985) offers an accurate portrait of the various components of an upper-class, British country

weekend, shooting driven game, circa 1913. The impressions conveyed are:

a. Shooting is an elite pastime.

b. British sporting traditions encourage talent among amateurs; however, active competition while shooting is not gentlemanly.

c. Active competition in shooting, trying too hard, can have tragic results.

16. *In the Blood* (1989) is a commercial documentary of an African safari which attempts to explain why sport hunting is a durable and honorable sport. This film takes off the gloves in its defense of sport hunting in Africa by using attractive participants who follow the rules of fair chase religiously, showing the male bonding rituals between young neophytes and older veteran hunters and evoking the historical memories of Theodore Roosevelt who conducted perhaps the most famous African safari in history (1909) with his son as a collector of specimens for various natural history museums. The film also portrays the uncompromising standards applied by honorable trophy hunters in their search for the largest specimens. The economic contributions to the economies of African nations promoting sport hunting from fees, licenses and other expenses paid by hunters are emphasized. One episode has the hunting party apprehending a party of poachers who were illegally killing animals in order to market the meat. A recurring theme is that sport hunters truly love and respect the animals they attempt to kill. The strong emotions produced by a successful stalk and kill are discussed and shown. The impressions conveyed are:

a. Sport trophy hunting can be an honorable and harmless activity when conducted according to the highest standards in pursuit of non-endangered species.

b. The best thing that can happen to a species whose habitat is threatened or whose life is forfeit when poachers are not controlled is to become a valuable trophy species.

17. *A River Runs Through It* (1992) weaves a celebration of fly-fishing, with all of its rituals, disciplines and elegance into a bittersweet story of one brother's attempts to rescue his younger brother from bad habits and dangerous companions. The shared "passion for waters" among the father and sons of this fly-fishing family is the anchoring theme to which the film returns repeatedly. The impressions conveyed of this aquatic blood sport are:

a. Fly-fishing is a high calling with many strictures and hard-won skills.

b. Fly-fishermen are led to travel to some of the most beautiful settings on earth in pursuit of their prey.

c. The world's cares and crimes are erased from consciousness while fishing.

## AMBIVALENT/NEUTRAL PORTRAYALS OF HUNTING

The following group of films display ambivalence regarding hunting. In several of them, the main character hunts in his early years but decides later in life that there are much better ways to spend time. For example, the hunter may unintentionally experience the presumed emotions associated with becoming the hunted prey. In other films in this group, attractive main characters display unattractive behaviors while engaged in hunting activities. These films suggest there exist many reasonable doubts about the legitimacy of hunting.

18. *Hunter's Blood* (n.d.) portrays a group of men drinking and carousing as they embark on their annual deer hunt in the Ozarks. When the hunters stop to replenish their beer supply, they irritate some local citizens. At the hunting grounds, they encounter a gang of poachers who attempt to destroy the hunters. The impressions conveyed are:

a. Hunters typically go hunting so that they can engage in behaviors they are not permitted or do not permit themselves back home.

b. The wilderness is a dangerous place, often because of other humans.

19. *The Most Dangerous Game* (1932) portrays two big game hunters who end up hunting each other on an island. The hero is a famous hunter who is shipwrecked on an island owned by another big game hunter who has gone mad as a result of his obsession with experiencing the thrill of the hunt. He seeks ever more crafty prey and decides that man as prey is the ultimate challenge. His obsession is only gradually revealed to the hero who is forced to take the role of prey, thus experiencing for the first time those possible feelings of terror felt by the hunted animals. The implication seems to be that hunters who experience what it is to be hunted will, perhaps, rethink their position. The general impressions conveyed by the film are:

a. Hunting can be a dangerous obsession, leading the hunter to antisocial lengths.

b. Hunters with prosocial characters will recognize the danger of their sport if shown the other side of the issue, the side of the prey.

20. *Man Hunt* (1941) portrays a famous English big game hunter who enrolls his hunting skills in a campaign to assassinate Hitler. He fails and is pursued, thus being called upon to use his hunting skills to evade his pursuers. The impressions conveyed by this film are:

a. Hunting skills can serve socially beneficial purposes (participation in a just war).

b. The hunter hero becomes the prey, thus experiencing some of the emotions of the pursued animals.

21. *Home From the Hill* (1960) portrays a father-son conflict in which the father, a skilled and noted hunter, wants his son to develop the same skills in order to enter manhood. The son develops the skills but ultimately rejects hunting as a false test of manhood. The impressions conveyed are:

a. Hunting is a male masculinity ritual.

b. Other and better ways exist to display what it means to be a man.

c. Skilled hunters are also skilled in sexual matters.

22. *Naked Prey* (1966) portrays an ivory hunting party in Africa at the turn of the century attacked by natives and taken captive. All but the hero are slaughtered. The hero is turned loose to flee on foot as long as he is able. He successfully eludes his pursuers. The impressions conveyed are:

a. The hunter can experience the feelings of a prey who is pursued by forces more powerful than he.

b. Hunters can experience feelings of great respect for their prey when the prey eludes them.

23. *The Last Safari* (1967) portrays an African white hunter who decides to give up hunting after one last trip. He pursues an elephant who killed his best friend. When he finally finds the elephant, he lets the elephant live. The impressions conveyed are:

a. Love of hunting is a phase in the lives of younger hunters which will pass for those who have the "right stuff."

b. The sadness at the death of animals reported by many hunters can become so overwhelming that it finally cancels out all the joy of the chase.

24. *The Deer Hunter* (1978) shows an annual deer hunting party as an important ritual of a male friendship group. The main character values his hunting skills and finds them useful when he is captured in VietNam. When he returns home, however, he finds he has lost his desire to kill. The impressions conveyed are:

a. Hunting skills are useful in warfare.

b. Battle experience lessens the desire to hunt because of the association of the death of human soldiers with the death of animal prey.

c. Giving up hunting is a meaningful symbol of one's desire for peace among humans.

25. *Dances With Wolves* (1990) portrays a U.S. Army officer during the Civil War learning to understand and value the culture of the Native Americans he is sent to supervise. Because the officer is cut off from contact with the military for a long period of time, he has an uninterrupted opportunity to join the Indians in various typical activities such as a buffalo hunt. Although the hunt is utilitarian, intended to produce food and materials for various tools and objects of Indian everyday life, the officer experiences the exhilaration of the chase and the kill. The impressions conveyed are:

a. Political correctness is demonstrated in the film credits which carefully reassure the audience that no animals were actually killed during the making of the film. The hunting scenes were staged to recreate the cultural practices of the Indians. Hunting animals to death is not acceptable in the current age.

b. Hunting for food can be exciting as well. The excitement, however, must be only a derivative consequence of the search for food.

## ANTI-HUNTING FILMS

The last group of films to be examined offers unequivocal condemnation of the forms of hunting they portray. No socially redeeming virtues are found for hunting in this group.

26. *King Solomon's Mines* (1950) portrays sport hunting only in the opening minutes. The hero is a safari white hunter, leading clients into big game fields. The client hunters are portrayed as blood-thirsty, excitable shooters of noble beasts whose majesty deserves more expertise and appreciation. The hero becomes

disgusted with the shoddy sportsmanship shown by his clients. One clumsily shoots an elephant which later charges the hunter and his gun bearer. The gun bearer is trampled trying to protect the client. The hero returns from the hunt fed up with his profession. The impressions conveyed by the film are:

    a. Professional hunters have a deep respect for the animals they pursue.

    b. The typical visiting hunter is a bumbling incompetent who is not worthy of the role he has temporarily purchased.

    27. *Bambi* (1942) is the classic animated film whose characters are all charmingly anthropomorphized. This picture offers the most effective condemnation of hunting for sport or any other reason that I have ever seen. I do not recall my childhood reactions to the story; however, I cannot imagine how any child could have positive feelings toward "hunters" after viewing it. The script is so understated but ominous when the subject of the dangers of the meadows and forests is explained to Bambi. Then, when the hunting season commences, the animals are subjected to the terror of constant bombardment by guns or hounds of the chase. No human hunters are ever shown, just their violent effects as animals flee, are hit or barely escape by their headlong flights. Then careless hunters loose another terror upon the animals— fire! The impressions conveyed are:

    a. Hunters are the agents of pure evil and boundless terror in the lives of the innocent animals.

    b. No one can understand why humans desire to pursue and kill the innocent creatures who do the humans no harm.

    28. *Track of the Cat* (1954) portrays the hunt for a stock-killing mountain lion. The character most obsessed with the hunt is a brutal, violent man who eventually dies from an accident caused by careless behavior induced by his obsession with the hunt. The impressions conveyed are:

    a. Hunting is most enjoyed by those with unsavory personalities.

    b. Hunting can induce obsessive behaviors.

    c. The prey of hunters are often cunning, malevolent forces in nature.

    29. *The Last Hunt* (1956) portrays professional buffalo hunters in the American West. The hero becomes repulsed with the slaughter of the buffalo and withdraws from the business while

the other main character becomes ever more obsessed with the successful killing of the animals. He eventually dies as a result of his obsession. The impressions conveyed:

a. Hunting/killing stimulates obsessive-compulsive behaviors.

b. People of good character eventually tire of hunting.

c. Hunting is ultimately disgusting to those who pursue it extensively.

30. *Roots of Heaven* (1958) has the hero trying to organize resistance to the slaughter of elephants in French Equatorial Africa. He organizes, essentially, a terrorist campaign against those humans who have any connection with the death of elephants: ivory dealers and a big game hunter. The impressions conveyed by this film are:

a. Big game hunting is destroying entire species.

b. Violent measures against other humans are justified in pursuit of protection for hunted animals.

31. *Shalako* (1968) portrays a British hunting party visiting the American West. The characters are boorish, bloodthirsty and unsporting. The impressions conveyed are:

a. The sporting code is easily disregarded by those nominally committed to it.

b. Big game hunting is a sport appealing to unpleasant personality types.

32. *Bless the Beasts and the Children* (1972) has as heroes a group of boys at a Western camp who attempt to stop a "hunt" organized to reduce the population of a local buffalo herd. The impressions conveyed are:

a. Opposing hunting is a noble activity.

b. Innocent youth understand the immorality of hunting better than do their elders.

33. *The Last Dinosaur* (1977) has as its main character a wealthy big game hunter who has tired of all earth has to offer in terms of prey. He encounters the opportunity to hunt a surviving member of an extinct species of dinosaur in a "hidden world." He and his party travel there, fail to kill the dinosaur and suffer severe losses to their numbers in the process. The big game hunter decides to stay in this new/old savage world and continue to pursue this most challenging prey of all. The impressions conveyed are:

a. Hunting is mainly a sport for the wealthy.

b. Hunting can become an all-consuming passion.

c. The dedicated trophy hunter has an insatiable urge to add new heads to his collection.

d. The dedicated trophy hunter is likely to feel that the world cannot comprehend his interest and thus moves on without him.

34. *Wolf Lake* (1979) tells the story of an annual hunting trip by four men who are flown into a lake camp. There they find their guide is absent and in his place are a young couple who provoke the hunters: the man because he was a VietNam deserter after being in combat, and the woman because she is not married to the man and because of her attractiveness. The hunters gradually escalate their aggressions toward the young couple who fight back until only they are left. The impression conveyed is that hunting situations easily lead to hunters forgetting civilized norms and behaviors.

35. *Heart of the Stag* (n.d.) is an Australian film with one main character who is an overbearing wife abuser, a father who forces incest upon his daughter and a passionate hunter of red deer stags. His daughter is rescued by the hero but, as the father attempts to thwart that rescue, he is gored and killed by a red deer stag. The impression conveyed is that passionate hunters are likely to be antisocial creatures who engage in some of the most despicable behaviors.

36. North Dallas Forty (1979) has a brief episode in which the professional football player characters are bird hunting in Texas. They engage in various pranks which typically discredit the hunter: shooting signs, shooting from a car, using a gun recklessly. The impressions conveyed are:

a. Hunters often revert to juvenile behaviors as part of the male bonding rituals typical of hunters.

b. Hunters are easily tempted to reckless behaviors when no one is around to police them.

37. *Southern Comfort* (1981) portrays Cajun trappers and fishers in Louisiana as persons with very savage temperaments when provoked. The film suggests that:

a. Subsistence hunters are much more prone to violence when provoked than are urbanized people.

b. The values and norms of subsistence hunters are "beyond the pale."

38. *Harry and the Hendersons* (1987) is a gentle tale of big game hunter whose family injures a Sasquatch (Big-Foot) while returning from a hunting trip. The family takes the Sasquatch

home, thinking it dead. Instead it revives and proceeds to affect their lives in various ways. One thing it hates is the killing of wild animals. Whenever it sees a stuffed hunting trophy, it attempts to give the animal a "decent burial." The hunter gives up his hobby in the end to please the Sasquatch. The impressions conveyed are:

>a. Hunting is disruptive to nature which would announce that fact if it but had a voice.

>b. Hunters who give up this recreation move to a higher level of environmental understanding, thus improving their characters.

39. *The Bear* (1989) offers as its main character a cute, orphaned bear cub who is adopted by an adult male grizzly bear. The adventures of the two bears brings them into contact with hunters who are collecting bear skins for commercial reasons. The final scenes show the male bear cornered by the hunter who in turn becomes the hunted; however, the bear refrains from pressing home its attack. The story is thoroughly anthropomorphic, attributing human-like emotions, virtues and behaviors to the bears: courage, mercy and protection of the weak. (In fact, solitary adult male bears, even the biological fathers, are most likely to cannibalize any cubs that remain in their vicinity.) The impressions conveyed are:

>a. The hunting of animals which have been anthropomorphized usually seems to the audience to be like hunting other humans. It appears vindictive and wantonly destructive.

>b. Hunters can learn honor, mercy and other noble virtues from observations of their prey.

40. *White Hunter, Black Heart* (1990) is a murky story of a famous movie director who agrees to make a film in Africa so that he can fulfill his dream of hunting big game. He becomes obsessed with hunting elephants and endlessly delays beginning the film until his obsession is resolved. This happens when he comes face to face with his prey and some seemingly noble act by the elephants wakes him from his dream-like pursuit and brings him back to the job at hand. He never kills the elephant. The impressions conveyed are:

>a. Sport hunting can easily become obsessive-compulsive behavior which consumes the hunter, causing him to put aside all other responsibilities to himself and others.

b. With good luck the obsession will be resolved and the hunter will come to his senses and resume normal responsibilities.

c. The attractions and pleasures of hunting are dangerous to sanity.

## ANALYSIS OF FILM DATA

These 40 films span over half a century and when they are classified by decade in terms of their anti-, ambivalent/neutral or pro-hunting messages, the following table results:

### VALENCE OF HUNTING THEMES BY TIME PERIODS

|        | PRO-HUNTING | MIXED | ANTI-HUNTING | TOTAL |
|--------|-------------|-------|--------------|-------|
| 1930s  | 2           | 1     |              | 3     |
| 1940s  | 3           | 1     |              | 4     |
| 1950s  | 2           |       | 5            | 7     |
| 1960s  | 3           | 3     | 1            | 7     |
| 1970s  | 1           | 2     | 5            | 8     |
| 1980s  | 5           |       | 3            | 8     |
| 1990s  | 1           | 1     | 1            | 3     |
|        |             |       |              |       |
| TOTAL  | 17          | 8     | 15           | 40    |
|        | (42%)       | (20%) | (38%)        | (100%)|

These data reveal that 58 percent of the films reviewed are anti- or ambivalent in the ways they portray hunting. Looking at the distribution of the dates of these films, we see that other-than-positive portrayals of hunting are found in all decades of the past half century, although they seem to be especially prevalent in the 1950s, 1960s and 1970s. As a proportion of all films within a decade, the 1940s witnessed the most favorable treatment of hunting, followed by the 1930s and 1980s. The 1990s so far have not produced any pro-hunting images on film and only the one pro-fishing film tallied earlier.

## CULTURAL SOURCES OF ANTI-HUNTING THEMES IN FILMS

The most recent data reveal that sport hunting was practiced by 18.5 million Americans in 1990 (Statistical Abstract, 1992: 241). It seems less than a random event, therefore, that such a relatively popular sport has been portrayed in a positive manner in the fictional film medium only slightly more than 1/3 of the time.

What could account for this apparently systematic pattern? Let us appeal to the thoughts of William Tonso who has postulated a significant dichotomy in popular cultures in America. On the one hand we have the "cosmopolitans" who live, work and participate in urban environments extremely removed from the rural environs which are the context for sport hunting. The cosmopolitan world view tends to anthropomorphize nature and natural things and reacts to "consumptive" uses of nature as acts of immorality akin to cannibalism. In this view, if natural things have rights like human beings, then each category deserves the absolute protection against violations of those rights. On the other hand, Tonso contends that "bedrock" Americans are guided by a world view which is practiced in more rural settings and includes the "consumptive" use of nature.

The production of fictional films is mostly controlled by the "cosmopolitans" and reflects their conceptions of the popular pastimes of the "bedrock" citizens. The substantial proportion of portrayals of hunters as negative characters undoubtedly plays some role in fostering and maintaining anti-hunting sentiments in the general population.

## ALTERNATIVE PORTRAYALS OF SPORT HUNTING?

Can nothing be done? Must those who enjoy hunting and respect its rituals and rules be eternally misunderstood, misrepresented and maligned by film makers? (Fishers have had a champion raised up in their cause recently with the release of *A River Runs Through It* [1992].) There are various portraits of sport hunting in literature which celebrate its more noble/honorable traits. I encourage attempts to bring episodes to the screen from any of the following works: *The Old Man and the Boy* (Robert Ruark), *The Bear* (William Faulkner), *Green Hills of Africa* (Ernest Hemingway). They offer a rich array of themes: mentoring, male bonding, courage under stress and environmental awareness. I recognize the difficulty of rendering on screen the essentially internal, psychological rewards which accrue to the successful hunter. If film makers were sympathetic, however, I am confident their creative juices could erode the obstacles to such portrayals. The "out-of-body" exhilaration that humans experience in the throes of sexual pleasure has been effectively developed in film. Perhaps film workshops could address the challenges that accompany the portrayal of the hunting act. The challenge would be no greater than the challenges inherent in the portrayal of any physical activity such as football, basketball, baseball, skiing, boxing, track. These activities have all been the basis for successful fictional film treatments.

If various types of hunting were portrayed more sympathetically, one more "minority" group could relax somewhat and be assured of a continuing place in our pluralistic society.

# Chapter Nine

**"As the Twig Is Bent:"**
**Hunting and Fishing Themes**
**in Late 19th- and Early**
**20th-Century Boys's Books**

## INTRODUCTION

Hunting and fishing as sports were owned by the European aristocracy and preserved for them by law (Cross 44). Poachers continually challenged this domination by taking game whenever and wherever it offered itself. Laws provided draconian penalties for violators who had the misfortune to be apprehended.

In the New World of North America, wildlife was so abundant that there seemed to be no need to restrain or regulate its consumption. Transplanted aristocrats and poor immigrants alike could consume what they liked by whatever means they liked (Cross 46).

From roughly the 1850s to 1900 the railroads, population growth, urbanization, refrigeration and abundant game stocks on the fringes of "civilization" provided the stimulus for wholesale, widespread market hunting and fishing. The market hunters operated from two cultural assumptions:

> ...the old belief in the freedom of the hunter in harvesting nature's bounty; and the belief in the freedom of any private enterprise, a belief which led us to see the world in commercial terms and to make the wild life a commodity of exchange no different from livestock. (Kimball and Kimball 92)

Because the patrician sportsmen sensed that their game stocks were threatened with depletions, the old class war was reignited. Upper- and middle-class, urban sportsmen lobbied long, hard and eventually successfully for laws to protect, preserve, conserve remaining game stocks for the perpetual enjoyment of the sporting community. Gradually market gunning and fishing came under control, but only after many game species were drastically reduced in numbers. (Loss of wild habitat was a major factor in these declines as well as market hunters and fishers.) Ex-market hunters became poachers outside the law or often

**134**

guides for urban sportsmen who could pay. Thus the distinctions of the served and the servers remained. The Kimballs offer a succinct summary of the fate of the commercial hunter:

> The full freedom of the American hunting tradition (unregulated) was destroyed when the hunter began feeding a nation instead of just his family—when hunting became a business. (91)

The Lacey Act (1900) was the turning point in ending the commercial trade in game species of animals and fishes. Sportsmen's organizations must be assigned credit for curtailing market hunting and fishing by means of their "moral crusade" (Becker 151). As part of this crusade, they constructed and articulated sporting codes of fair chase rules, adopted from English sporting norms and rituals, for honorable hunters and fishers to impose on themselves: practice proper etiquette in the field; have knowledge of the pursued game and its habitat; develop skills with the tools of the chase so that they are used with precision and coolness; give game a sporting chance to escape; possess an aesthetic appreciation of the whole context of sport that included a commitment to its perpetuation (J. Reiger 22, 26).

First articulated by Henry William Herbert, a transplanted English sportsman in the late 1830s, these rules of proper conduct in the sporting field were promoted relentlessly in articles and on the editorial pages of the young sporting outdoor magazines of the day (*American Sportsman* est. 1871; *Forest and Stream* est. 1873; *Field and Stream* est.1874; *American Angler* est.1881). A host of highly visible public figures, most from upper class backgrounds, enlisted in the fight to protect game stocks, wild habitats, forests, etc.: Theodore Roosevelt, Charles Hallock, George Perkins Marsh, Seth Green, George Bird Grinnell, William Hornaday, Charles Wesley Powell, John Burroughs, John Muir, Charles Sheldon, Gifford Pinchot and later Aldo Leopold.

The code of sporting ethics they espoused remains the guiding light of the hunting and fishing fraternity. (A recent check of articles dealing with the ethics of hunting and fishing over the past decade revealed that 80 percent or more appeared in the outdoor sporting press.) As the Kimballs observe, however,

Unfortunately, hunters are not all sportsmen. Some are unethical, rude, destructive, ignorant law violators. Too often hunters are judged by the misconduct of the worst. A cut fence or fine shot in the hind quarter of a cow leads to the erroneous conclusion that hunting brings forth the base, primitive nature of man. It is often said that a normal, decent citizen reverts to a destructive, ruthless Mr. Hyde when he gets a gun in his hands. But a gun does not change the nature of a man. If he is an unscrupulous hunter, he also kicks his golf ball out of the rough and is a crooked lawyer or a cheating plumber. Hunt with a man for a day and you will know whether or not you want to do business with him or have him as a friend. The crude hunter, the spoiler, will always be with us, but because he violates the rules of the game he cheats himself. The rewards of true sportsmanship are great. The gentleman hunter, respecting the rights of others and following the rules of the game which give his quarry better than an even chance, knows the reward of being a sportsman. (123-24)

## CHILDREN AND OUTDOOR RECREATION

Reiger contends that at the turn of the present century:

...costing nothing, the outdoors was free to rich and poor alike, and...nineteenth century youth, especially males took full advantage of its possibilities. Fishing in early boyhood and hunting in adolescence seem to have been almost universal. (J. Reiger 42-43)

However, adult attitudes about the legitimacy of these activities were changing gradually, perhaps because of the efforts of the sportsmen's organizations:

In the early part of the century purely recreational angling and gunning, even for juveniles, was still frowned upon in the North, but the same "thaw" in the compulsive practicality of Americans that helped sportsmen benefited boys everywhere; more time could now be taken up with hunting and fishing without fear of censure or punishment. In the South youngsters escaped for the most part the puritanical heritage of their Northern counterparts. Although fishing was never as popular there as in the North, hunting, even for recreation, always seems to have been a central part of the socialization process for males. (J. Reiger 43)

## BOYS' ADVENTURE BOOKS

The question this chapter addresses is to what extent did literature for boys reflect the changing attitudes about wildlife and its pursuit by sportsmen as leisure/sporting activities? If literature mirrors the times in which it is produced, then the themes of the adventure stories for boys should serve as a barometer for the course of elite-driven public opinion of the times. A subtext of the chapter is the early appearance of anti-hunting propaganda in children's books. Before we zero in on specific themes, however, we must establish the general context of children's literature being produced.

> Every age has felt the need to provide new instructions in its children's books on how life is to be lived. Thus children's books do not merely reflect the contemporary social scene and the problems of adult life; the simplified manner in which they present their subjects also makes them something of magnifying glasses. (Orvig 40)

America emerged from the Civil War as a nation experiencing rapid growth of literacy, increasing material standards of living due to industrialization, a growing leisure class whose recreations were admired and copied by the masses when they could afford to do so, and swelling ranks of immigrants who waited their turn at the bottom of the socioeconomic ladder. The leisure classes consisted of those who had "worked and won" in this land of opportunity, unlike the Continental leisure classes whose inherited fortunes wore the patina of age.

Literature created for children is a relatively recent addition to humankind's literary productions. This literature reflected the cultural values of the parent generation who purchased this literature for their children. The themes were designed to entertain as well as instruct young readers regarding the world view which comforted those in charge. Therefore, if we follow the changing course of these themes through time, we may find that they parallel the changing values, interests and concerns of the surrounding culture.

Events which excited the adult community—the wars, exploration in unknown parts of the world, the exploration of the western frontier and conflicts with and among the contending forces—were themes which are prominent in the literature of the 1850-80 period.

From 1880-1900, stories for children (mostly boys) concentrated on the sports available in the non-urban places: hunting, fishing, exploring. The boy characters associate with the remnants of a earlier era—old scouts, hunters and trappers who introduce them to a taste of life as it was. Also, during this era, we find young boys associating with famous historical figures— explorers, military leaders. A bland history lesson was delivered along with the excitement. This era also produced the Alger books whose heroes struck it rich in the urban wilderness by means of a touch of luck and an abundance of virtue which enabled them to seize the "main chance" when it wandered by.

From 1900-15, the salient themes shifted to adventures with the technological marvels of the day. The exciting new inventions—especially automobiles, airships and electricity—were the occasions for boy heroes to sally forth and accomplish some thrilling goal or overcome some adversity. Additionally, organized, professional sports and books of college life and collegiate sports were widely popular. The "western," in its nearly modern form, was invented during this period and found ready acceptance among youthful fantasizers.

From 1915-20 World War I intruded significantly in themes in boys' adventure stories. Many of the new inventions of war, tanks, airplanes, boats, ships and motorcycles were mechanical characters in these stories, either as heroes or villains.

From 1920-40 the stories move to anthropomorphized animal heroes, detective stories, and stories of spies and intrigue during the late, great War to end them all. Also a number of western heroes entered the literature, sometimes originating in the forms of comic books: the Lone Ranger, Red Ryder, Tarzan. Sports stories also increased in proportions among themes.

Some very few series were devoted to hunting and fishing (Big Game Series), but most successful series of stories for boys used the various themes which had been successful in other series (since many different series were often produced by the same writer or publisher, i.e., the Stratemeyer Syndicate). As the author of *Rascals at Large* observed regarding the formula for books about kids:

> The formula for a book about kids, unless the protagonists were specialists like Tarzan, the Hardy Boys, or Baseball Joe, was a simple one. A series always centered around a small town, except that at least once in each series a boy had to

transfer his activities out West, once to somewhere full of ice and snow, once to the jungle full of animals and unregenerate natives, and once aboard ship. The rest of the time he could lounge around the house or one of the boarding schools that seemed to exist everywhere at that period. The hero had a small group of cronies who accompanied him everywhere. There was always a fat boy, an athletic boy, and a rib-tickling joker. There was also a bully, accompanied by two or three toadies, who moved heaven and earth to irritate our heroes. The bullies, oddly enough, appeared wherever the protagonists happened to be, even if it were the headwaters of the Amazon. Of course the boys achieved whatever Bluebird of Happiness they had been pursuing, and the bullies were either shelved for the next book or reformed by contagious exposure to honor, goodness and truth. (Prager 218-19)

In other words, hunting was one of the adventures with which boys could identify, along with school sports, exploration, war and inventions.

## BOYS' ADVENTURE BOOKS:
## HUNTING AND FISHING THEMES

My sample of books spanned 80 years (1869-1949) and consisted of two types: series books roughly conforming to the formula offered above and stories with characters who appeared only in single titles. The latter type offered by far the best story plots and the best writing in my opinion. I will refer to the books by date of publication in order to assess whether the evolution of sporting ethics in hunting and fishing reached into the themes appearing in boy's adventure books across the 80-year span of titles.

The first book in my sample, *The Boy Hunters* (1869) by Capt. Mayne Reid, uses the theme of productive leisure in its story line. Three brothers from Louisiana travel to the prairies of the West to kill a white buffalo for their father so that he can honor a promise to a friend to supply a mounted specimen for a European museum. Many adventures with wild animals are had along the way. No mention is made of game laws or fair chase or other sporting rituals later constituting the sportsman's code.

The second title, *The Camp in the Foothills* (1881) by Harry Castleman, continues this theme of productive leisure. The good boy in the story is studying to become a taxidermist. He travels to the West with a commission from a museum back East to collect specimens for display. The hero shows remorse at having to kill an antelope but no sympathy for wolves he encounters. The book delivers a good deal of moralizing about honesty, keeping one's word and correcting past mistakes for the sake of honor.

The third title, *The Rod and Gun Club* (1883) by Castleman, has the heroes offer criticisms of market hunters on the Chesapeake Bay, claiming the laws against "looting" (puntgunning) are not enforced because the market hunters retaliate. Late in the story the "club" members, on holiday from the prep school they attend, travel for a hunting and fishing vacation in Maine. They discover the joys of fishing for trout with light tackle rather than heavy rods. The characters affirm the necessity of observing game laws and offer criticisms again of "pot-hunters." The laws of Maine at the time allowed night hunting of deer with lanterns. The main character shoots a large moose at night by that means. Then he worries that the moose season had already ended and contacts the warden to pay any fine owed.

The next two titles, *Through Forest and Fire* (1891) by Ellis, and *Frank Meriwell's Hunting Trip* (1901) by Burt Standish, do not express clearly any values concerning hunting sportsmanship. They both take the main characters through exciting adventures, with narrow escapes, and the Good triumphs at the end.

Three titles from the *Boy Hunters Series*, published in 1906-08, begin to push boy fantasy adventures and depart from more realistic story lines. In these three titles, *Four Boy Hunters, Guns and Snowshoes* and *Young Hunters of the Lake* written by Captain Ralph Bonehill (a.k.a. as Edward Stratemeyer), the good boys are allowed by their parents to travel to nearby wilderness areas, equipped with a rifle, shotguns and pistols. There they together hunt animals, shooting at them in volleys and killing multiple members of various species at one time: squirrels, quail, ducks, deer. The successful boy hunters send most of their game back to town to their parents or to be sold, thus endorsing the theme of productive leisure. The boys lament that game is disappearing and suggest that more protective laws are needed or no game will remain in 15-20 years. Once the question is raised about whether they are shooting too much game. They decide, "If we don't, someone else will." The boys discuss the idea of ending deer hunting for two years to let the game numbers recover. The good boys compete with a rival group for numbers and sizes of game animals shot. The boys talk about being careful with fire in the woods. But they take a carbide lamp with them for night hunting. Comment also is made about how the forests are threatened by lumbermen.

*Tom Swift and His Electric Rifle* (1911) by Victor Appleton is barely worth mentioning. This fantasy tale has the hero and friends traveling to Africa in an airship to collect ivory with the marvelous rifle which used electrical charges as projectiles. The whole point is the search for profit with no sporting values demonstrated or discussed.

*Bart Keene's Hunting Days* (1911) takes its heroes to New York State's lumber wilderness. The heroes discuss the hunting laws which prohibit hunting deer when a "tracking snow" is present. They seem to follow this rule carefully. This book was written by Allen Chapman who essentially recycled the same theme in the next title.

Chapman's *Tom Fairfield's Hunting Trip* (1915) sends the good boys on a hunting trip for deer head trophies to the New York Adirondacks. The heroes observe the following principles: no killing just for fun, no shooting at any target you are not sure of, no wasting of meat. One of the good boys has decided not to hunt but to photograph animals instead.

The next two titles by Eliot Whitney (a.k.a. H.L. Sayler) appeared as parts of the *Big Game Series* (for boys). *Mankiller of the Foothills* (1912) and *The Giant Moose* (1912) are adventure fantasy tales of boys seeking dangerous animals who have harmed loved ones. Exciting adventures are experienced along the way in both books. Little or no explicit affirmations of sporting values are offered. The justification for the hunting in these stories is the redress of grievances against the hunted animals as dangerous forces of nature.

The single title in my sampling dealing with fishing, *The High School Boys Fishing Trip* (1913) by H. Irving Handcock, offers mixed messages concerning sporting ethics. The boy heroes express concerns about overfishing of angling waters and concerns about developers buying land and selling "bungaloos" to wealthy fishermen. On the other hand, the hoary theme of productive leisure is introduced when the boys catch trout to sell as well as for sport. One boy took 34 trout in an afternoon, later selling 100 pounds of brook trout to a hotel. The characters declare that no sportsman would take every last fish from a water; but they continue fishing a productive stream until the diminished catch suggests they are approaching depletion.

James Oliver Curwood published two titles in 1915: *The Wolf Hunters* and *The Grizzly King*. *The Wolf Hunters* takes two boys into the wilderness on a wolf-hunting and fur-trapping trip. Their main purpose is to take wolf-scalps for the government bounty paid on "varmints." The wolf remained a despised denizen of the wilds at that time and no sympathy was registered for the animals killed beyond delight in their commercial value. *The Grizzly King* is a curious story, almost autobiographical for the author, which details how the author-hunter pursued a giant grizzly into the British Columbian wilderness and gradually lost his desire to kill it. A much altered version of this story appeared in the recent film, *The Bear*. (See chapter 8.) The main theme of the book is how a dedicated hunter may gradually change his motivations for traveling to the wilderness. Communing with nature, enjoying the observation of the natural behaviors of wild animals, rather than seeking to capture and dominate those beings, are ideas the writer offers his readers. Although not purely an anti-hunting theme, it promotes the concept that the desire to hunt and kill may be an earlier stage of a person's interactions with the natural world.

The last two pre-World War I titles were also published in 1915 and written by Silas Boone. This author dedicated the entire series from which these two titles are drawn "...to teach the young reader how to protect himself against the elements, what to do and what to avoid, and above all to become self-reliant and manly." *Phil Bradley's Shooting Box* and *Phil Bradley's Snowshoe Trail* take place in two famous hunting areas. The first takes the heroes to Currituck Sound, North Carolina, for a duck-hunting outing. The boys endorse the necessity of hunting season laws for wildfowl. The boys scrupulously shoot only their legal limits of ducks. A "market hunter" character in the story turns out to be sending the ducks he kills to feed children at an orphanage. The second title takes the gang to Northeastern Canada, perhaps New Brunswick. The boys mention Teddy Roosevelt's African safari (1909), lambaste "game hogs," lament the growing scarcity of game, endorse legal limits on moose and applaud ethical hunting guides as law-abiding persons whose professional interests are served by abundant game for future clients. The central character is repeatedly described as tiring of being a hunter who kills and instead pursues a growing interest in wildlife photography. However, this leader understands the desire of others with less hunting experience to seek trophies. The leader admonishes his friends to avoid killing excess game when the opportunity presents itself, to shoot only when certain of killing an animal and to avoid causing any game animal unnecessary pain. Poor sportsmanship displayed by a rival camp of wealthy American hunters offers a counterpoint to the ethical pursuit of fish and animals by the heroes.

Animal stories, with anthropomorphized main characters, originated earlier than the examples appearing in my sample of boy's books. In fact, I suspect that the appeal of animal stories was/is likely as great, perhaps greater, for girls as for boys. Stories told from the perspective of animal characters permit obvious opportunities for anti-hunting themes when dealing with human relationships to animals. The predator animal characters are held blameless for doing what is natural in their pursuit of food. Humans are held responsible, however, for exercising the unnecessary choice of seeking to kill wild animals.

The first two examples of animal stories with anti-hunting themes came from the pen of Thornton W. Burgess. *Lightfoot the Deer* (1921) and *Blacky the Crow* (1922) involve adventures for the main characters with hunters who are eventually foiled in their deadly pursuits. In *Blacky the Crow* a human friend of the animals acknowledges that humans have the legal right to hunt but should not be unfair in their pursuit of game. The human boy decides to foil the duck hunter's efforts by scaring away the ducks before they reach the hunting blind of the real hunter. The real hunter spreads corn near his blind to lure the ducks his way. The boy claims "there ought to be a law" against such unfair behavior. Blacky the crow calls this "unfair" and claims that Reddy Fox and Old Man Coyote would never do anything so low in their pursuit of the little animals.

Now, let me introduce you to the pinnacle achievement in anti-hunting animal stories, *Bambi* (1929) by Felix Salten. May Hill Arbuthnot authored many editions of a flagship text in children's literature. Several generations of elementary school teachers gleaned their knowledge of children's literature in courses taught with this title as its text. In the third edition she presents the following analysis of *Bambi*, a popular animal story, animated by Walt Disney:

> ...The book is exquisitely written and the animals well characterized. They are all there, from little field mice and rabbits to foxes and great elk. There is also "He," the enemy of

all the forest creatures. His scent carries terror, his pale hairless face chills them with horror because just beneath it are 'legs' which reach out with a stick, and the stick shoots fires and death far beyond its reach. *Bambi* tells a story of man's hunting from the standpoint of the hunted and is therefore desperately tragic in places. The account of the hunters encircling the animals and then frightening them from their hiding places with terrible noises and constant shooting is so horrible it should make readers hate this barbarous practice.... (402)

The Disney film remains, in my estimation, the most effective piece of propaganda for anti-hunting I have ever encountered. The book is equally effective, although the plot is more complex than the Disney version. "Bambi" has long been the code word for loveable, anthropomorphized animals who are victimized by humans. I believe it fair to describe this book as playing the role for the anti-hunting movement which *Uncle Tom's Cabin* played for the anti-slavery movement or Rachel Carson's *Silent Spring* played for the environmental movement!

*Big Red* (1945) by Jim Kjelgaard, is a superbly written dog story which endorses observation of game laws but portrays nature as a harsh adversary who defeats all but the most hardy and well-prepared persons. The ethical behavior of hunters, both human and canine, is repeatedly affirmed in the story.

The last story, *Through Forest and Stream* (1949) by Duane Yarnell, is really a college sports story taken to the woods. The heroes and rivals attend a summer wilderness camp to learn "woodcraft and how to fish and trap and hunt." A cash prize is offered to the school represented by the best boy in each of these performance categories. Rules are set for the interpersonal competition among the campers but no mention is made of game laws or fair chase procedures. The ferociousness of wild animals is exaggerated by the author who apparently knows something about fishing but absolutely nothing about hunting.

## CONCLUSION

This subsample of books is but a fraction of those I must eventually examine; however, I find unmistakable effects on themes in boys' books of the two "moral crusades" concerning wildlife. Hunting and fishing for sport and leisure, practiced according to ethical and legal codes, were gradually accepted as legitimate pastimes by the adult community. This legitimacy is reflected in the boys' adventure stories; however, the sturdy idea of "productive leisure" repeatedly reappeared in the story lines.

The other moral crusade, which contends that hunting by humans is unnecessary and inhumane, has roots as least as old as the 1920s according to evidence from my sample. Theodore Roosevelt 20 years earlier, however, had already chastised those whom he described as "nature fakers" for misrepresenting the facts of nature. They were the writers at the turn of the century who used anthropomorphized animal characters in their stories. Roosevelt affirmed the Social Darwinian precept that man is part of nature and nature is "red in tooth and claw." This idea remains the guiding principle of those who celebrate humankind's moral and political perch atop the food chain (Causey; Vitali).

**Chapter Ten**
The Commodification
of Hunting and Fishing:
From Izaak Walton
to Instructional Videos

## INTRODUCTION

The commodification of leisure activities, including hunting and fishing, has only relatively recently engaged the attentions of "...many scholars in history, sociology, and mass communication, leisure, and cultural studies" (Butsch vii). In this last chapter I discuss commodification as it concerns hunting and fishing specifically. The general issues informing debate and research on the commercialization of leisure include the histories of various leisure activities as they allegedly have become commercialized as well as the contention over whether,

> As consumers of leisure products, have we lost control of our own free time? Does leisure represent the interests and values of participants—that is, is it an arena of self-expression? Or have capitalists or reformers designed leisure to control the behavior of lower classes? (Butsch 4)

What follows is a cursory history of the commodification (commercialization) of hunting and fishing over the past century and a half. My tentative conclusion regarding the debate over commercial leisure as social control versus self-expression is inferred from the historical examples which I have assembled. The evidence suggests to me, and I hope my readers, that "(c)onsumers participate in shaping new products and practices, which corporations in turn shape into profits and 'mass culture' " (Butsch 19).

The business of America and any capitalist system is business, seeking profits from commodity production and sales. For the purposes of my discussion, I will use "commodity" to mean an objectified bit of reality—artifact, service, relationship—which has exchange value in some market. A commodified activity is one in which I have to purchase something in order to participate: a license, special equipment, travel and accommodations, guidance on site and/or services of others upon completion of the commodified activity. Any one of these components makes an activity a commodity, in my judgement. The more components included, the more chances for additional profits for the commodity manufacturers/providers.

A final note: the history of the transformation of hunting and fishing from subsistence activities in America to packaged, guaranteed, commercially available experiences involves such a long time and so many threads of influence, that I find it ludicrous to pretend that there was anything intentional, contrived or predetermined about the process or outcome. The evidence suggests to me, to borrow a phrase from my statistical brethren, that the historical process of commodification was an additive/multiplicative and monotonic blend of the developments I shall describe.

There is no question, however, that contemporary hunting and fishing activities are highly commercialized, involving de facto partnerships between governments and private businesses in what is part of a world-wide, $3-trillion-per-year entertainment and tourism industry (PBS, 23 March 1993). A recent business analysis of hunting in the U.S. reported that hunters spend more the $10 billion each year on their pursuit of all kinds of game (Farnham 80). (The evolution of hunting and fishing technologies and their impacts on standards of sportsmanship were discussed in earlier chapters.)

## BEFORE THE BEGINNING

Hunting and fishing were subsistence economic activities among the earliest European arrivals to North America. When agriculture provided the economic base for our ancestors, hunting and fishing remained recreational sports which achieved two valued outcomes: productive leisure. These sports were to be had by stepping outside the farmhouse door and retiring to the woods, fields or waters in the neighborhood. As long as citizens had access to the wild sporting habitats through their own relatively slight efforts, no commodification was present: no licenses, trespass fees, guides, special equipment or other purchases were necessary. This was home-made sport carried out with home-made equipment or tools with multiple uses, i.e., firearms for personal protection and/or civilian militia uses.

## IN THE BEGINNING

I have argued repeatedly in earlier chapters that humans need no persuading to take part in activities which involve the pursuit, outwitting and domination of other life forms since humankind evolved as a hunting species. All sports besides hunting and fishing engage some one or a combination of the hunting acts: running, pursuing, jumping, evading, aiming, throwing and "killing." The challenge of any substitute sport/recreation is to lead the player to discover satisfactions which derive from participation. Therefore, no one had to convince humans that hunting and fishing delivered emotional reinforcements, when hunting and fishing became more difficult to pursue.

As urban and industrial settings absorbed more and more of the populations of America and sporting habitats (woods, fields and waters) were lost to development or pollutions, the traditional desires and rituals of hunting and fishing retreated farther beyond the reach of ordinary citizens. The middle and upper economic classes had the means to secure the earliest forms of commodified hunting and fishing experiences. It may have begun with the fantasies of hunting and fishing adventures which were fueled by the narratives printed in early sporting journals of the 1830s such as *Spirit of the Times, The Cabinet of Natural History and American Rural Sports* and *American Turf Registry and Sporting Magazine* (Weidner 13-14). They printed letters from literate sportsmen who extolled the sporting opportunities in various parts of America and lectured readers on proper conduct in the sporting field. Henry William Herbert (Frank Forester), an expatriate Englishman, led the efforts in the 1840s and 1850s to transplant the sporting codes of the upper class British sportsman to the fields, woods and waters of his new homeland.

William Elliot's *Carolina Sports by Land and Water* (1859) put another log on the fires of hunting and fishing fantasies of his readers. "Wealthy planters such as Elliot sought to emulate, to engage, and to surpass Old World aristocrats with their privileges and refinements in field sports" (Marks 18). The sporting community always seems willing to imitate the sporting fancies and styles of the social echelons above them. In sum:

Before the Civil War, sportsmen were few. They kept in touch by reading and contributing to *The American Turf Registry* and *Spirit of the Times*. These periodicals reprinted the English sporting codes and provided images for American converts to the "proper world of field sports." After the Civil War, the spread of urbanization and industrialization, together with changes in transportation and weapons, made getting back onto the land and to nature attractive for many Americans.

Sportsmen shared a particular worldview defined by attitude, motivation and affiliation. Sportsmen tracked their quarries in a highly stylized manner, conversed with a technical vocabulary explicit about game and guns, demonstrated an abiding interest in natural history, adhered to a code of ethics, donned fashionable dress afield, often professed an interest in highly trained dogs, and belonged to cosmopolite associations. Only certain mammals were worthy to test the skills of a sportsman and his dog. These prey were to be taken in a highly refined manner. Deer were given ground to exercise their natural instincts for escape, and birds were taken only on the wing. (Marks 46)

These idealized sportsmen provided the fantasy to be pursued by those who aspired to the field sporting life. But what of those who possessed the personalities but not the bulging purses of these elite sportsmen?

William Murray published *Adventures in the Wilderness: or Camp-Life in the Adirondacks* in 1869. This book generated a new sporting tourist industry for the Adirondacks, Catskills and Poconos of the Northeast. The urban populations of the eastern states could find wilderness retreats only several hundreds of miles from their crowded cities (Weidner 16). A sportsman of modest means could now buy access to hunting and fishing without having to own the habitats.

All during the period being examined, hunting and fishing fantasies were fed and teased by producers of sporting art. Nathaniel Currier and Currier and Ives issued more than 140 titles related to hunting, trapping, camping, wild animal studies and dead-game life. These prints sold for about 25 cents to 3 dollars, and were thus within the budget of an average family. (Weidner 21)

For the more prosperous families, painters such as Arthur Fitzwilliam Tait produced hunting and fishing scenes as well as wildlife studies which evoked the sporting and natural history possibilities of wild places nearby.

In the 1870s and 1880s, specialized magazines began publishing which were devoted only to hunting and fishing. *American Sportsman* (1871), *Forest and Stream* (1873), *Field and Stream* (1874) and *American Angler* (1881) fed the fantasies of the sporting communities with stories of sporting adventures, editorials promoting the sporting codes of ethics and lobbying against the continuation of market hunting, and the earliest discussions of the necessity of habitat conservation (Weidner 14). These magazines also assisted the commodification process by advertising the latest commercially manufactured equipment and offers of places to go and guides to hire to carry out the readers' hunting and fishing fantasies. In short, these magazines reflected existing interests (self-expression of the readers) and reinforced these interests with information about what to buy and where to go.

Advice about commercially available hunting and fishing opportunities was so popular that elaborate guidebooks were compiled and offered for sale, often as publishing adjuncts of the sporting magazines. Of course, "treatises on field sports date back at least to Xenophon; Dame Juliana Berners and Sir Izaak Walton carried a long tradition into the modern age" (Hardy 82). The guidebooks I refer to include Charles Hallock's *The Fishing Tourist: Angler's Guide and Reference Book*, published in 1873 and devoted to salmon and trout fishing techniques, equipment and locales. Hallock also published *The Sportsman's Gazetteer and General Guide* in 1877. This was the "mother" of all guide books in that it aspired to provide the reader with a guide to

> the game animals, birds and fishes of North America: their habits and various methods of capture along with copious instructions in shooting, fishing, taxidermy, woodcraft, etc. together with a directory to the principal game resorts of the country; illustrated with maps. (Hallock)

These exhaustive and exhausting instructions consumed almost 700 pages and were compiled by *Forest and Stream* magazine which Hallock edited and published. This guide also identified the most convenient forms of transportation to the resorts. The newly booming railroads were frequently mentioned.

A decade later, *The Sportsman's Guide to the Hunting and Shooting Grounds of the United States and Canada* was compiled and edited by William C. Harris, editor of the *American Angler.* This guide covered much of the same information as did Hallock's; however, the emphasis was on railroad transportation. An index of transportation companies listed over 200 railroads and several steamship companies. Each company had pages specified which described the sporting opportunities which could be reached on its line. Thirty-seven railroads purchased ads in Harris's guide elaborating on their services (I-XV). Many of the ads offered additional guidebooks detailing places to go, places to stay, people to hire and sporting adventures to be had by traveling on their railroad. Here is an illustrative entry in Harris's guidebook from Ohio.

> Napoleon (Wabash R.R.)—For turkey and partridge 8 miles south, and for deer 11 miles southwest; quail are also found and are with partridge the most abundant; Oct. to Jan. 1 best; double team $4 per day; hotels $2 per day; no trained dogs or professional guides; country—wooded and open: owners usually do not object; shooting excellent. (151)

The 1880s witnessed other contributions to the continued idealization and commodification of hunting and fishing sports. The Boone and Crockett Club was organized by elite American sportsmen, including Theodore Roosevelt, in 1887 to promote the sporting ethic, the study of natural history of the prey species and to work to preserve those species in perpetuity by working to eliminate market hunting. This national organization of prominent sportsmen was a continuation of the process begun in the previous decade which witnessed the formation of amazing numbers of hunting and fishing clubs which purchased or leased habitats for the propagation of their sports.

> As early as 1874, (George Bird) Grinnel (sic) printed in Charles Hallock's journal, *Forest and Stream*, editorials that vehemently protested wholesale slaughter of the nation's wildlife. During the next winter (1875), in response to the editorials and arising out of the simmering discontent with wildlife destruction, nearly a hundred sportsmen's clubs, ten or twelve state groups and one national association formed to propagate wildlife. Four years later (1879) the number of sportsmen's clubs had tripled to 308. (Altherr 13)

The hunting games of trap and skeet gathered momentum during the decade of the 1880s, graduating from live birds as targets to artificial ones. During this decade Theodore Roosevelt began publishing narratives of his hunting trips in the American west. Of course, these writings became more popular after he ascended to the Presidency at the turn of the century. The 1880s also saw the further development of guns and ammunition, rendering both less expensive, more reliable and more heavily advertised.

The 1890s continued the trends of the previous decades and ended with the passage of the Lacey Act in 1900. This act greatly reduced the profitibility of market hunting and marked the beginning of the end of wild game as a commodity to be produced/harvested by the commercial hunter for resale. Shortly thereafter, wild game was reserved permanently for the sportman's use. This accelerated the evolution of the hunting and fishing experiences as commodities by guaranteeing that there would be wild game to pursue. By the turn of the century, however, hatchery fish and pen-raised birds increasingly were a part of the sporting landscape.

## MID PASSAGE

In the first decade of the 20th century, the sporting magazines, equipment manufacturers, railroads and steamship lines continued to advertise the sporting commodities they marketed. In the realm of fantasy enhancement, Theodore Roosevelt left the Presidency and took a long hunting and collecting safari in East Africa (1909), which he documented in *African Game Trails* (1911). The public seemed fascinated with his reports and children's books and toys were commercial spinoffs from his trip. Stewart Edward White, a best-selling American author in this century's early decades, also helped to popularize the idea of the African safari with his safari narratives, including *African Campfires*, *Land of Footprints*, *Lions in the Path* and at least one novel, *Back of Beyond*.

White was not alone with his encouragement of hunting fantasies. Other novelists lived and wrote about the consumptive uses of wildlife. Jack London, James Oliver Curwood, Rex Beach and especially Zane Grey, produced fictional and factual portraits of hunting and fishing adventures around the world (Nye; G. Reiger, *Zane Grey*).

The Johnsons, Martin and Osa, in the 1920s and 1930s, pioneered wildlife motion pictures which featured hunting encounters with African game to thrill commercial audiences. Those nature/travelogue/hunting films are direct ancestors of the video tapes of the 1980s and 1990s which have had such a major impact on hunting and fishing practices and are so popular at present. But more about this later.

In the 1930s Ernest Hemingway contributed to the safari fantasy with his narrative, *The Green Hills of Africa* (1934). Several of his short stories inspired Hollywood movies in the 1940s and 1950s which had African safari themes, including *The Macomber Affair* (1947) and *The Snows of Kilimanjaro* (1952) (see ch. 8).

Rider Haggard's *King Solomon's Mines* (1885) is perhaps the best known of the stories of Africa which made it to the screen. This story has been filmed seriously three times, in 1920, 1938 and 1950. An interesting sidelight to Haggard's work is the intriguing possibility that Haggard's fictional idealization of the great white hunter, Allan Quartermain, may have been drawn from the real-life hunter, Fredrick Selous. However, Haggard's books were so widely read throughout the world that life may have imitated fiction in later generations of hunters and safari clients who may have modeled their behaviors and expectations on Haggard's hero. Allan Quartermain has always been much better known than Fredrick Selous. The commodification of this image or stereotype is evidenced by the fact that Haggard's work remains in print to this day.

The hunting of African game is of special interest in our discussion of commodification. The African hunt as commodity began as a means to harvest valuable products such as ivory. According to Bartle Bull, however:

> By 1900, it was no longer the day of the lonely eccentrics, the pioneer, unpaid hunters who lived for the free, wild life of the hunt. The new hunters were visitors, essentially on a sporting holiday, and many needed local experts to plan their expeditions and lead them in the field. (Bull 127)

> The desire to establish one's manly credentials in the field, and especially to be respected by one's professional white hunter, is often the most important trophy a client seeks on safari.... Later white hunters came to perceive that this manly affirmation is a valuable commodity to be sold to their clients, in some cases with great skill and profit. (Bull 182)

While I am discussing Africa, let me emphasize that current hunting conditions illustrate a point stressed in chapter 3, the interaction of technology and standards of sportsmanship.

Commodification of prey species, like technology, exhibits complex interrelationships with other issues. The animal rights' movement abhors hunting and wishes that animals be protected because of their trans-species rights. Technology has made possible the profitable commodification of the African hunting experience: weapons, means of travel. Technology has also made possible the widespread decimation of wild animal species for perhaps another set of selfish reasons. Let me invite Bartle Bull to assist by quoting his observations regarding one hunting habitat:

> By 1983 the Sudan, Africa's largest country, was in chaos. Civil war flared again between north and south as Muslim fought black and the government sought to impose Muslim law on the Christian and animist tribes of the southern Sudan. Undisciplined troops and armed gangs roamed the country, ravaging villages and slaughtering the game with automatic weapons. Gone were the old days of artful hunting, when the Dinkas of the Sudan used bow traps, digging holes containing hidden triggers that released snares of twisted buffalo hide up the legs of passing elephants that stumbled into them. (Bull 325)

In sum, technology and commodification are neither inherently moral or immoral. The uses to which they are put are choices by human agents, the ultimate architects of morality.

Returning to the United States, the federal and state governments throughout this century have contributed to the process of commodification of hunting and fishing by their actions. Fish and game departments of state governments have been largely financed by license sales to hunters and fishers. These agencies have worked diligently, if not always wisely, in developing and managing habitats and game populations for their sportsmen constituents. The anti-hunting and animal rights advocates have scathingly characterized state wildlife departments as working only for the interests of the consumptive users of wildlife.

The federal government, for its part, has enacted legislation at various times which has aided and abetted commodification. In 1929 the Migratory Bird Conservation Act authorized the acquisition of land for waterfowl refuges. In 1934 the federal waterfowl stamp was established as a revenue source for the purchase of new waterfowl refuge areas. In 1937 the Pittman-Robertson Act, with the sportsmen's blessing, imposed an 11 percent excise tax on sporting arms and ammunition to be used "to cover 75% of state costs for cooperative programs in wildlife research, management and development" ("Hunting Controversy" 59). The wildlife refuge program of the federal government aids commodification because "hunting is allowed in 262 of the nation's 466 wildlife refuges" ("Hunting Controversy" 64).

Government involvement in the hunting and fishing commodities has played a critical role because:

> Private commercialization is inhibited by the costs of acquiring, developing, and maintaining the physical setting, but government spending on parks and recreation areas—for campgrounds, trails, roads, lakes—creates the conditions required for the private accumulation of capital in recreation-related industries. (Greer 152)

The development of industrial capitalism, leading to higher wages, more disposable income and shorter work weeks has witnessed even working class families spending more money on non-necessary items such as leisure activities. From 1875 to 1918 working class families increased the proportions of their incomes spent on non-necessary items, including recreation, from less than 10 percent to roughly 25 percent (Butsch 14).

> This rate, sustained even through the Great Depression, had increased by the 1980's to over 40% as Americans shifted from "time-intensive" to "goods-intensive" recreation. (14)

## TO THE PRESENT

All of the previously identified forces which have contributed to the commodification of hunting and fishing remain intact and continue to metasticize: more products, more places to go, more assistance in getting there. Allow me to elaborate a bit.

Since World War II, the interstate highway system has provided new opportunities for the sportsperson to travel hundreds of miles to distant sporting grounds or waters. The airlines industry increasingly provides access to sporting opportunities in the far-flung corners of the globe. I described my own limited sampling of those opportunities in an earlier chapter. I am on a variety of mailing lists of sporting travel companies who offer access to hunting and fishing adventures for a price on all five continents. The exotic locales described in the hunting-travel narratives of the past century can be revisited by today's sportsperson, with bargain rates for non-hunting/fishing companions. Here is just a recent sample from my mailbox.

*Canada North Outfitting Inc.* has me on its mailing list because I was a customer of several commercial hunting trip enterprises while doing the research for this book. Their catalogue for hunts and safaris in 1993 includes the following opportunities around the world, with prices for the actual hunt. (Transportation, trophy fees, taxidermy fees, shipping fees for trophies, gratuities for guides, all are extra expenses.)

| LOCATION: | GAME SPECIES | HUNT DURATION | COST |
|---|---|---|---|
| RUSSIA and other | Snow sheep | 10 days | $13,000 |
| countries of C.I.S.: | Marco Polo sheep | 17-21 days | $27,000 |
| Tadzhikistan, | and ibex | | |
| Kirghisia, | Urial | 8 days | $13,500 |
| Turkmeanian republic | Tur | 5 days | $ 6,100 |
| Afghanistan, Siberia | Brown bear | 6-10 days | from |
| Dagestan, Kazakhstan | | | $ 4,500 |
| | Siberian roe deer | 7 days | $ 2,500 |
| | Saiga antelope | 3 days | $ 2,900 |
| | Asiatic wapiti | 4 days | $ 4,000 |
| | Pacific walrus | 6 days | $ 6,500 |
| CZECHOSLOVAKIA: | Red deer stag | 5 days | $ 3,800 |
| | Mouflon (sheep) | 5 days | $ 3,800 |
| | Wild boar | 5 days | $ 2,500 |
| CHINA: | Blue sheep | 4 days | $ 7,900 |
| | Forest game | 8 days | $ 3,600 |
| NEW ZEALAND: | Tahr and chamois | 7 days | from |
| | | | $ 2,500 |
| | Red deer | 5 days | from |
| | | | $ 2,000 |
| SCOTLAND: | Red deer | 6 days | $ 3,000 |
| | Red grouse | | $900 per day |

AFRICA:  A long list of trophy fees for each species in each country is included in the catalogue.

South Africa,
Zimbabwe,Botswana,

| Tanzania | Buffalo | 7 days | $ 5,600 |
| | "Crop raiding" elephants | 10 days | $11,000 |
| | | | (includes trophy fees) |

Various plains species from $185 to $600 per day with minimum booking periods in some places.

These listings are illustrative of the thriving commerce of world-wide hunting adventures for sale. Similar listings are available for fishers.

Special-interest organizations with national memberships have multiplied in the past 25 years and joined the older groups committed to preserving sport hunting and fishing. A partial list includes: Duck's Unlimited, Whitetails Unlimited, Quail Unlimited, Pheasants Forever, Trout Unlimited, Salmon Unlimited, Wild Turkey Federation, Elk Foundation, International Game Fish Association, Boone and Crockett Club, Pope and Young Club, Safari Club International, Bass Anglers Sportsman Society. These are just American organizations.

In a major way, the commodification of the prey species, whether mammal, fish or fowl, is *the* means to protect those species. The best protection under current cultural practices is to establish a species' value in terms of economic impact resulting from maintenance of its habitat and access to it by licensed consumptive users of wildlife. Protection through commodification is especially important in Africa today. Sporting tourist dollars typically provide major portions of foreign exchange flowing into those countries which allow hunting of species protected from poachers and other encroachments of civilization (Bull 326).

Various popular game species have been restored to old habitats and introduced into new ones, thus creating the justification for special licenses whose revenues support the restoration/introduction activities: more game, more licenses, more game.

Old technologies have been widely resurrected, i.e., archery and primitive firearms (see chapter 3) and special seasons created to encourage their use. More waters have been officially labeled as trout streams which has unleashed a host of special restrictions, such as no live bait, no barbed hooks, catch-and-release-only areas.

Mail-order marketing, a resurgent phenomenon of the 1980s, parades a plethora of specialty products for hunters and fishers including "how-to," "where-to" and "use-these" advice. The hunting and fishing television shows have emerged in the last two decades, first achieving national prominence with ABC's *American Sportsman* show. The medium continues today in more local or regional programming and on cable channels, occupying non-prime-time slots in the schedules. These programs are frequently continuous commercials for products featured by the program personalities (performers).

In addition, the VCR revolution of the last decade has done a great deal to sustain hunting-fishing experiences as commodities. Urban populations are less and less likely to develop the skills and attitudes appropriate to hunting and fishing as normal parts of childhood socialization. Instructional videos are especially suited to the schedules of today's outdoors sportsperson. These videos offer condensed experiences in the field which, through judicious editing, allow a "bottom-line" approach. The exciting conclusions of fishing/hunting trips can be witnessed by fast-forwarding or, for the more patient viewer, by waiting out the half-hour-to-hour-long narratives. Of course, these video adventures are subject to the temptations of "nature-faking" which Theodore Roosevelt and his peers decried at the beginning of this century. The editing process can make wildlife sequences extra cute, extra sad or just thoroughly anthropomorphic. The true nature of hunting and fishing experiences cannot be conveyed in most cases.

On the other hand, I have an acquaintance locally who has shared his library of hunting videos with me. This hunter is the epitome of the ethical, self-disciplined sportsman. He uses the videos to refresh his memory regarding size, shape, sounds and movements of his prey species. He has initiated his wife, a sociologist colleague of mine, into the hunting "brotherhood" by analyzing with her the video tapes, annotating the video commentaries as they watch them together. He has been such an effective teacher that during her first season in the field his wife collected the largest whitetail buck either has ever seen. Last season, under his tutelage and that of the video tapes, she collected a buck with both the bow and muzzleloading rifle. The videos remain an important part of their yearly preparations for the hunting seasons.

For the more affluent sportsperson, personal instruction in field skills are available at seminars offered on fly fishing, bird shooting and dog training, among others. Orvis and L.L. Bean are examples of companies organizing these skill-for-sale experiences. (They parallel golf seminars and summer camps for younger athletes in an ever-burgeoning variety of activities, including baseball, football, basketball, tennis, swimming, soccer, hockey and jogging.)

## INTO THE FUTURE

While hunting (and perhaps fishing) remains a multi-billion-per-year industry, its future is clouded. As I prognosticated at the end of chapter 7, trophy hunting, the least accepted form of sport hunting by the general public, is most likely to endure because of its commodified status and, relatedly, because of the depth of the pockets of its most ardent practitioners. Ironically perhaps, I close this chapter and this book with thoughts and words drawn from a recent survey of hunting as a business which appeared in *Fortune* magazine. After completing his swift perusal of "what's hot and what's not" in hunting circles in terms of animals pursued, equipment purchased and means of arranging access to hunting habitats, Farnham consults his crystal ball and sees this future for hunting:

Antihunters nip its heels daily now, sometimes drawing blood. Organizations such as the Fund for Animals have legally blocked the hunting of the grizzly bear and bison in Montana, mountain lions in California. Meantime hunters are losing a more crucial battle: one for kids' attention. Who needs hunting when you've got Nintendo? Manufacturers lament the fact that hunters, both as a market and as individuals are maturing.

Not only have hunters done a crummy job selling the sport's virtues to the unconverted; by ceding moral ground to opponents, they have spread the belief than no virtues exist. But they do. Advocates cite hardihood, camaraderie, and conservation. But few mention its greatest social function: re-grounding human carnivores.

With every passing day, more Americans hold a view of nature informed by Disney movies...They feel uncomfortable connecting animals with food....

## 160  Hunting and Fishing for Sport

Hunting cures all such illness by exploding sentimentality. In the moment a hunter pulls the trigger, he takes responsibility for an act other meat eaters pay someone else to do. By killing, he willingly couples himself into the chain of life and death binding all other predators and prey. And thus bound, he experiences nature in a way far more intimate than whale watching. He watches it and then eats it.

Hunters provide an inconvenient reminder that man's elevator, evolutionally speaking, remains stuck between floors—above beasts, but a good way below angels. When hunters hunt, they confirm their animal status. Though everywhere the forces of uplift strive to deny man's heritage, hunters embrace it...they sense they're a little out of step. But that doesn't mean they're about to go quietly. (86)

# Notes

### CHAPTER ONE

[1]Although hunting and fishing are treated together in this chapter, significant differences divide them as sporting activities and as activities to worry environmentalists. A brief excursus of these differences will be useful. Both hunters and fishers seek to find and capture live animals. Hunters, however, seldom have the option of being successful and allowing the animal to live. Even when the hunter has the animal in his sights and chooses not to squeeze the trigger or release the arrow, there is always the chance he would have missed or wounded the animal and not brought the hunt to a successful conclusion. A fisher, however, can maintain the option of conquering his prey and allowing it to live (catch-and-release), assuming it is not injured. As the trout fishers' creed declares, "a trout is too valuable to catch just once." Also, few laypersons anthropomorphize fish as they tend to do with "Bambi" or other cuddly forms of game.

Sportsmanship is less controversial in fishing. The fish is thought to have a "choice" whether or not to bite a bait or lure. In fishing there is no pursuit and no alleged, provoked fear on the part of the prey as in the case of hunted, land-living game. Unfair means exist, of course, for the pursuit of fish: dynamite, electric shock, poison.

Curiously, with land-based game, sportsmanship requires the quickest and most humane means of dispatching the object of the hunt. With fish what is defined as most sporting is to bring the fish to bag (net) with the lightest, most fragile tackle which maximizes the fish's opportunities to escape. Also, and most curiously, the thrill of fishing is agreed by many to derive from the sensations of struggle which are transmitted to the "hunter" via the sensitive tackle. Few defenders of wildlife seem inclined to define the fish's struggles as a source of torment and pain which so offend the defenders of land-based wildlife.

Another factor which favors fishing over that of hunting land animals is that standard fishing equipment makes no noise and poses no danger to the general population as do the tools of the hunter. The fly rod, spinning reel and bass boat cannot contribute to social mayhem as can the rifle, shotgun, pistol and even the bow and arrow. The fisher is stereotyped as a gentle, harmless pursuer of a productive sport. (For a dissenting view, see McClanahan 2.) No novels, films or television documentaries portray the fisher as dangerous, demented, environmentally unsound.

Perhaps one other critical distinction between the hunter and fisher is that the prey of the latter is unseen and does not overtly beautify the landscape as do water fowl, game birds, deer. While the nature-lover-environmentalist assumes that fish reside beneath the surface of lake, river or stream, constant reminders are not present. Additionally, the habitat approached by the fisher is not the object of intense incompatible competition for use as game lands. Farmers, hikers, nature watchers are threatened by activities of hunters. Fishers, however, utilize waters inhabited by swimmers, skiers, boaters, who, in fact, are a substantial threat to fishers' success. An area of water can be exploited more intensely by fishers, without mutual interference, while hunters usually cannot collect in time and space and pursue their sport except perhaps in waterfowl hunting or battues (drives) for deer pheasants, boar.

[2]See Kelly for a more extensive discussion of definitions of sport, recreation and leisure and their interrelationships.

[3]Competition is present, however, in certain branches of these activities in the forms of trophy hunting and international scoring of the "heads" killed as well as fishing tournaments where numbers and size of fish netted or boated are criteria for awards. More remotely, competition in hunting and fishing occurs among the equipment users: target shooting and fixed and moving artificial targets (skeet, trap, sporting clays, running boar and deer) and fly and bait casting tournaments which offer competition in distance and accuracy. Entertainment to bystanders may be provided by some of these contests.

[4]Since the organization conducting the survey is publicly supportive of hunting, there is reason to suspect that those organizations who participated may have tempered their answers. No mention is made of how these organizations happened to be included in the survey sample. These data, therefore, must be taken as illustrative rather than definitive of the variations in attitudes about hunting among the population of such organizations. The following organizations were listed as declining to participate in the survey:

The Explorers Club
Friends of Animals
Game Conservation International
Humane Society of the United States
International Society for the Protection of Animals
IUCCN
Shikar-Safari Club International

[5]The topics of hunting and fishing have been and are being studied, as the references herein document, but only by a handful of sociologists. The studies done by non-sociologists consist largely of attitudes of hunters, the meanings of the activity to them and the attitudes of non- and anti-hunters toward this activity. Researchers of these topics range from scholars in schools of forestry and environmental studies (Kellert) to students pursuing degrees in natural resources (W. Shaw). Much of the work has been commissioned by wildlife departments. The thrust of this corpus of research has been to increase understanding between hunters and non or anti-hunters. The motivation for such research is strictly applied. These sponsors have a vested interest in serving hunters while fending off the concerted attacks of their opponents (W. Shaw 45-48). Only a few sociologists have been uncovered so far, with work completed on either hunting or fishing: Atamian, Bryan, Dargitz, Gill and Hummel and Foster. Perhaps other sociologists have conducted work in these areas. If so, their work has only found outlets in forums obscure to me.

[6]I have no empirical evidence of this assertion. Perhaps, instead, work in these areas is not submitted to the higher status journals.

## CHAPTER 2

[1]The following analysis benefited greatly from "Hunting Controversy" (1992). See this reference for an extended treatment of these issues.

[2]For an extended and enlightening philosophical discussion of the dispute over sport hunting, see Loftin; Causey; Vitali; and King.

## CHAPTER 3

[1]See Mannix, 1967, for a discussion of other hunting methods.

[2]For a summary of arguments and descriptions of some groups which embrace such a view, see chapter 2. Also see D. Shaw, 1973: 3-41. For a sample of primary sources of this view, see Amory; Caras; Duffy; Krutch.

## CHAPTER 4

[1]An earlier version of this chapter was coauthored with Dr. Gary Foster, a colleague and dear friend. We published that version in the *Journal of Leisure Research*. Dr. Foster has graciously permitted me to rewrite our joint effort to fit with the contents of this book. Of course, I relieve him of any shared responsibility for mistakes which might appear in the current version.

[2]For a broader consideration of the transformation of "work forms" into "play forms," see Stone.

[3]For a more general treatment of self-imposed obstacles or handicaps as the essence of sport or play, see Miller.

[4]For a sense of the dramatic increase in fisherwomen as a separate population, see Henschel, 1984.

[5]The larger organizations (e.g., B.A.S.S.) promote national tournaments, facilitating the emergence of professional sport anglers. For example, the 1983 B.A.S.S. fishing tour awarded more than $1.4 million in cash and prizes and culminated in the $100,000 B.A.S.S. Masters Classic. Professional sport angling is facilitated by corporate sponsorship of the pros, i.e., backed by lure, line, tackle, engine, boat manufacturers and other companies benefiting from exposure through pro sport fishing (Henschel 43).

[6]In 1990, Larry Nixon of Bee Branch, Arkansas, won the most prize money. As of 1990, Nixon's lifetime earnings as a pro bass angler were over $600,000 (Rooney and Pillsbury 95). Ken Cook won over $150,000 in 11 months, the most won by any angler in a single year (Henschel 43).

## CHAPTER EIGHT

[1]This chapter would have been impossible without my having access to the film collection of Prof. Sarkis Atamian, Dept. of Sociology (ret.) University of Alaska at Fairbanks. I visited with Prof. Atamian and his wife during two summers and we spent countless happy hours viewing many of these films which I have not been able to locate elsewhere. Prof. Atamian and I were unable to share in the drafting of this chapter; however, he contributed his comments on an earlier draft. Our discussions of hunting, fishing and trophy seeking were centrally formative in my analysis of these films as well as in other sections of this book. THANK YOU SARKIS!

# BIBLIOGRAPHY

Allison, Col. *The Trophy Hunters.* Dust jacket. New South Wales, Australia, 1979.

Altherr, Thomas L. "The American Hunter-naturalist and the Development of the Code of Sportsmanship." *Journal of Sport History* 5.1 (Spring 1978).

Amory, Cleveland. *Man Kind?* New York: Dell, 1974.

Appleton, Victor. *Tom Swift and His Electric Rifle.* New York: Grosset and Dunlap, 1911.

Arbuthnnot, May Hill. *Children and Books.* 3rd. ed. Scott, Foresman, 1964.

Atamian, Sarkis. "The Social Psychology of Non-subsistence Hunting." Paper presented at the 32nd Alaska Science Conference, American Association for the Advancement of Science, 1981.

B.A.S.S. *Handbook for Members of the Bass Anglers Sportsman Society of America.* Montgomery, AL: B.A.S.S., 1984.

Barness, John. "Grand-slams Flim-flams and Record Book Bunco." *Field & Stream* 96 (May 1991).

Becker, Howard. *Outsiders: Studies in the Sociology of Deviance.* New York: Free, 1963.

Bender, David L., and Bruno Leone. *Animal Rights: Opposing Viewpoints.* San Diego, CA: Greenhaven P Inc., 1989.

Bernard, Luther L. *Instincts: A Study in Social Psychology.* New York: Holt, 1924.

Blackmore, Howard L. *Hunting Weapons.* New York: Walker and Company, 1971.

Boddington, Craig. "Big Game Hunting Preserves." *Peterson's Hunting* 10.1 (Jan. 1983).

Bonehill, Captain Ralph (Edward Stratemeyer). *Four Boy Hunters.* New York: Cupples & Leon, 1906.

_____. *Guns and Snowshoes.* New York: Cupples & Leon, 1907

_____. *Young Hunters of the Lake.* New York: Cupples & Leon, 1908.

Boone, Silas. *Phil Bradley's Shooting Box.* New York: New York Book Co., 1915.

_____. *Phil Bradley's Snowshoe Trail.* New York: New York Book Co., 1915.

Bradbury, Basil C. "Texas Safari." *Peterson's Hunting* 10.1 (Jan. 1983).

Brandner, Michael. *Hunting and Shooting: From the Earliest Times to the Present Day.* New York: G.P. Putnam's Sons, 1971.

_____. *The Hunting Instinct: The Development of Field Sports Over the Ages.* London: Oliver and Boyd, 1964.

Bristow, Allen P. *Rural Law Enforcement.* Boston: Allyn and Bacon, 1982.

Brokaw, Howard P., ed. *Wildlife and America.* Council on Environmental Quality. U.S. Government Printing Office, 1973.

Brusewitz, Gunnar. *Hunting.* New York: Stein and Day, 1969.

Bryan, Hobson. *Conflict in the Great Outdoors.* Birmingham: Bureau of Public Administration, U of Alabama, 1979.

_____. "Leisure Value Systems and Recreational Specialization: The Case of the Trout Fisherman." *Journal of Leisure Research* 9.3 (1977).

_____. "The Sociology of Fishing: A Review and Critique." *Marine Recreational Fisheries.* Ed. Henry Clapper. Washington, D.C: Sport Fishing Institute, 1976.

_____. "Spring-stream Flyfishermen: Management Implications of a Specialized Leisure Subculture." Paper presented at the American Fisheries Society Symposium on Human Behavior Aspects of Fishery Management, Honolulu, HI, 1974.

Bull, Bartle. *Safari: A Chronicle of Adventure.* London: Viking, 1988.

Burdge, Rabel J. "Levels of Occupational Prestige and Leisure Activity." *Journal of Leisure Research* 1.3 (1969).

Burgess, Thornton W. *Blacky the Crow.* New York: Grosset & Dunlap, 1922.

_____. *Lightfoot the Deer.* New York: Grosset & Dunlap, 1921.

Butsch, Richard, ed. *For Fun and Profit: The Transformation of Leisure into Consumption.* Philadelphia: Temple UP, 1990.

Cameron, William Bruce. *Informal Sociology.* New York: Random House, 1963.

Campbell, Bernard G. *Humankind Emerging.* 2nd ed. Boston: Little, Brown, 1979.

Campbell, Frederick. "Participant Observation in Outdoor Recreation." *Journal of Leisure Research* 2.4 (1979).

Caras, Roger. *Death as a Way of Life.* Boston: Little Brown, 1970.

Cartmill, M. "Four Legs Good, Two Legs Bad." *Natural History* (Nov. 1983).

Castleman, Harry. *The Camp in the Foothills.* Philadelphia: John C. Winston, 1881.

_____. *The Rod and Gun Club.* Philadelphia: Henry T. Coates, 1885.

_____. *The Young Waterflowers.* Philadelphia: John C. Winston, 1885.

Catton, William R., Jr., and Riley E. Dunlap. "The Use of Leisure and Its Relation to Levels of Occupational Prestige." *American Sociological Review* 21.5 (1978).

Causey, Ann S. "On the Morality of Hunting." *Environmental Ethics* 11 (Winter 1989).

Chapman, Allen. *Bart Keene's Hunting Days.* Cleveland: Goldsmith, 1911.

_____. *Tom Fairfield's Hunting Trip.* New York: Cupples & Leon, 1915.

Circle, H. "Angling: New Gear for '85." *Sports Afield* Dec.1984.

Clarke, R.C. "Social Sciences, Social Scientists, and Wildlife Management." *38th Federal Provincial Wildlife Conference Transactions*, 1974.

Colberg, Donald Arthur. "Moral and Social Values in American Adventure: *Adventures for Boys*, 1865-1900." Diss. U of Minnesota, 1973.

Conway, William J. Review of *Handbook of Social Science of Sport.* Eds. Gunther R.F. Luschen and George H. Sage. *Social Forces* 61 (1982).

Cross, Gary. *A Social History of Leisure Since 1600.* State College, PA: Venture Publishing, 1990.

Curwood, James Oliver. *The Grizzly King.* New York: Doubleday Duran, 1915.

_____. *The Wolf Hunters.* New York: Grosset & Dunlap, 1915.

Dargitz, R.E. "Disillusionment with a Fantasy? The Relative Impact of Massification on the Perception of Sport Fishermen." Paper presented at the Popular Culture Association Conference, Louisville, KY, 1985.

_____. "The Inter-relationships of Occupation, Job Satisfaction, Leisure Specialization and Role Commitment: An Exploratory Study of a Salmon Fishing Camp." Paper presented at the North Central Sociological Association Conference, Louisville, KY, 1985.

Denzin, Norman K. *The Research Act: A Theoretical Introduction to Sociological Methods.* Chicago: Aldine, 1970.

DiSilvestro, Roger L. *The Endangered Kingdom: The Struggle to Save America's Wildlife.* Wiley Science Editions. New York: John Wiley and Sons, 1989.

Ditton, R.B. "Recreational Striped Bass Fishing: A Social and Economic Perspective." *Marine Recreational Fisheries* 5. Ed. H. Clepper. Washington, D.C.: Sport Fishing Institute, 1980.

Duffy, Maureen. "Beasts for Pleasure." *Animals, Men and Morals.* Eds. Stanley and Roslind Godlivitch and John Harris. New York: Taplinger Publishing Co., 1972.

Dunlap, Roy F. "Metallic Silhouette Rifle Shooting." *The Book of Shooting for Sport and Skill*. Ed. Frederick Wilkinson. New York: Crown, 1980.

Ellis, Edward. *Through Forest and Fire*. Philadelphia: Henry T. Coates & Co., 1891.

Ellis, Lee. "The Decline and Fall of Sociology, a New Paradigm." *The American Sociologist* 13 (1977).

Evanoff, V. *The Freshwater Fisherman's Bible*. Garden City, NY: Doubleday, 1964.

Farnham, Alan. "A Bang That's Worth Ten Billion Bucks." *Fortune* 125 (9 Mar. 1992).

Fedler, A.J. "Elements of Motivation and Satisfaction in the Marine Recreational Fishing Experience." *Marine Recreational Fisheries* 9. Ed. R. Strond. National Coalition for Marine Conservation, 1984.

Fisher, Elizabeth. *Women's Creation: Sexual Evolution and the Shaping of Society*. New York: McGraw-Hill, 1979.

Flores, Dan. "The History of Man the Hunter." 1985. Printed in *Gun Digest Hunting Annual*. Northfield, IL, DBI Books, 1986.

Fox, Michael W. *Returning to Eden: Animal Rights and Human Responsibility*. City: Robert E. Krieger Publishing Co., 1986.

Fraleigh, W.P. *Right Actions in Sport: Ethics for Contestants*. Champaign, IL: Human Kinesics Publishers, Inc., 1984.

Garbrielson, I.N., ed. *The Fisherman's Encyclopedia*. Harrisburg, PA: The Stackpole Company, 1963.

Gates, Elgin. "Metallic Silhouette Pistol Shooting." *The Book of Shooting for Sport and Skill*. Ed. Frederick Wilkinson. New York: Crown, 1980.

Gerrare, Wirt. "Evolution of Sport with the Gun." *Outing* Sept. 1901.

Gill, Allan Duane. "The Social Circle of Catfishermen: A Contribution to the Sociology of Fishing." Thesis. Kansas State U, 1980.

_____. "Fishing as a Third-order Activity: Implications for Qualitative Sociology." Paper presented at the Southwestern Sociological Association Conference, San Antonio, TX, 1982.

Greer, L. Sue. "The United States Forest Service and the Postwar Commodification of Outdoor Recreation." *For Fun and Profit: The Transformation of Leisure into Consumption*. Ed. Richard Butsch. Philadelphia: Temple UP, 1990.

Hallock, Charles. *The Fishing Tourist: The Angler's Guide and Reference Book*. Franklin Square, NY: Harper and Brothers, 1873.

_____. *The Sportsman's Gazetter and General Guide*. New York: "Forest and Stream" Publishing Co., 1877.

Handcock, H. Irving. *The High School Boys Fishing Trip*. Philadelphia: Henry Attemus, 1913.

Hardy, Stephen. "Adopted by All the Leading Clubs: Sporting Goods and the Shaping of Leisure, 1800-1900." *For Fun and Profit: The Transformation of Leisure into Consumption.* Ed. Richard Butsch. Philadelphia: Temple UP, 1990.

Haresnape, Geoffrey. *The Great Hunters.* Cape Town. City: Purnell, 1974.

Harris, Marvin. *Cannibals and Kings: The Origins of Cultures.* New York: Random House, 1977.

Harris, William C. *The Sportsman's Guide to the Hunting and Shooting Grounds of the United States and Canada.* New York: The Anglers' Publishing Co., Charles T. Dillingham, 1888.

Hendee, John C., and Dale R. Potter. "Hunters and Hunting: Management Implications of Research." *Proceedings of the Southern States Recreation Res, Applications.* Asheville, NC. USDA Forest Service General Technical Report SE-9, 1976.

Henschel, T. "Bassing: Hook, Line and Sinker." *The Saturday Evening Post* July 1984.

Hinman, Bob. *The Golden Age of Shotgunning.* Prescott, AZ: Wolfe Publishing, 1982.

Hobusch, Eric. *Fair Game.* New York: Arco, 1980.

Hope, J. "The Well-lured Trout." *Science* Nov. 1984.

Huizinga, J. *Homo Ludens: A Study of the Play Element in Culture.* Boston: Beacon P, 1950.

Hull, Denison Bingham. *Hounds and Hunting in Ancient Greece.* Chicago: U of Chicago P, 1964.

Hummel, R.L., and G.S. Foster. "A Sporting Chance: Relationships Between Technological Change and Concepts of Fair Play in Fishing." *Journal of Leisure Research* 18.1 (1986).

"Hunters Helping to Feed the Hungry." *Times-Courier* 25 Sept. 1992. Charleston, IL: Associated P.

"Hunting Controversy." *Congressional Quarterly, Inc.* 2.3 (14 Jan. 1992).

International Game Fish Association. *World Record Fishes-1985.* Fort Lauderdale: I.G.F.A., 1985.

Jones, J.D. "Handguns: State of the Art." *Safari* 8.6 (Nov./Dec. 1982).

Kellert, Stephen R. "Attitudes and Characteristics of Hunters and Antihunters." *Transactions of the 43rd North American Wildlife and Natural Resources Conference.* Washington, D.C.: Wildlife Management Institute, 1978, 1979.

_____. "Perceptions of Hunting and Wildlife in America." *Hunting Magazine* Winter 1981.

_____. "Policy Implications of a National Study of American Attitudes and Behavioral Relations to Animals." Washington, D.C.: U.S. Government Printing Office, 1978.

Kelly, John R. "Leisure and Sport: A Sociological Approach." Luschen and Sage. Champaign, IL: Stipes, 1981.

Kimball, David, and Jim Kimball. *The Market Hunter*. Minneapolis: Dillon, 1969.

King, Roger J.H. "Environmental Ethics and the Case for Hunting." *Environmental Ethics* 13 (Spring 1991).

Kjelgard, Jim. *Big Red*. New York: Scholastic Book Services, 1945.

Koller, Larry. *The Treasury of Hunting*. New York: Odyssey P, 1965.

Krutch, Joseph Wood. "The Sportsman or the Predator? A Damnable Pleasure." *Saturday Review* 17 Aug. 1957.

Lathrop, Donald. "The 'Hunting' Economies of the Tropical Forest Zone of South America: An Attempt at Historical Perspective." *Man the Hunter*. Eds. Richard B. Lee and Irven De Vore. New York: Alldine, 1968.

Linder, S.B. *The Harried Leisure Class*. New York: Columbia UP, 1970.

Lipset, Seymour Martin, and Everett Carl Ladd, Jr. "The Politics of American Sociologists." *American Journal of Sociology* 78 (1972).

Loftin, Robert W. "The Morality of Hunting." *Environmental Ethics* 6 (1984).

Luschen, Gunther R.F. "Sociology of Sport: Development, Present State, and Prospects." *Annual Review of Sociology*. Eds. Alex Inkeles, Neil Smelser and Ralph H. Turner. Palo Alto, CA: Annual Reviews Inc., 1980.

Luschen, Gunther R.F., and George H. Sage, eds. *Handbook of Social Science of Sport*. Champaign, IL: Stipes, 1981.

Major, H. *Salt Water Fishing Tackle*. Rev. ed. New York: Funk and Wagnalls, 1948.

Mannix, Daniel P. *A Sporting Chance*. New York: E.P. Dutton & Co., 1967.

Marks, Stuart A. *Southern Hunting in Black and White: Nature, History and Ritual in a Carolina Community*. Princeton, NJ: Princeton UP, 1991.

Marsden, William. *The Travels of Marco Polo*. New York: Dell, 1961.

McClanahon, Timothy R. "Are Conservationists Fish Bigots?" *Bioscience* 40.1 (1990).

McFadden, J.T. "Trends in Freshwater Sport Fisheries of North America." *American Fisheries Society Transactions* 98.1 (1969).

McIntosh, P. *Fair Play: Ethics in Sport and Education*. London: Heinemann, 1979.

Menke, Frank G. *The Pictorial Encyclopedia of Sports.* Enlarged ed. Chicago: Progress Research Corporation, 1955.

Michener, James G. *Sports in America.* New York: Random House, 1976.

Miller, S. "Ends, Means, and Galumphing: Some Leitmotifs of Play." *American Anthropologist* 75.1 (1973).

Morgan, Elaine. *The Descent of Woman.* New York: Stein and Day, 1972.

Morris, Desmond. *The Animal Contract: Sharing the Planet.* New York: Warner Books, 1991.

_____. *The Naked Ape.* New York: Dell, 1967.

_____. *Manwatching: A Field Guide to Human Behavior.* New York: Harry N. Abrams, 1977.

New Buffalo Charter Service. Brochure. New Buffalo, MI, 1981.

"A new kind of business..." *Times-Courier.* Charleston, IL. 31 Mar. 1986: B12.

Nye, Russel. *The Unembarrassed Muse: The Popular Arts in America.* New York: Dial, 1970.

Ogburn, W.F. *Social Change.* New York: Viking, 1938.

Olson, F. *Successful Downrigger Fishing.* Tulsa, OK: Winchester, 1981.

Orvig, Mary. "One World in Children's Books?" *Top of the News* June 1972.

Parsons, J.W. "History of Salmon in the Great Lakes, 1850-1970." Technical Papers of the Bureau of Sport Fisheries and Wildlife. U.S. Department of Interior, Fish and Wildlife Service. Washington, D.C., 1973.

Prager, Arthur. *Rascals at Large.* New York. Doubleday, 1971.

Price, S. "New Chances for World Record Bass." *Bass Master Magazine* Sept. 1984.

Rathbone, St. George. *Campmates in Michigan.* Chicago: M.A. Donahue, 1912.

_____. *Rocky Mountain Boys or Camping Out in Big Game Country.* Chicago: M.A. Donahue, 1913.

_____. *The Young Fur Traders.* Chicago: M.A. Donahue, 1912.

Regan, Tom. *The Case for Animal Rights.* U of California P, 1983.

Reid, Mayne. *The Boy Hunters.* New York: American Publishers, 1869.

Reiger, George. "Hunting from Earliest Times to the Middle Ages." *The Complete Book of Hunting.* Ed. Robert Elman. New York: Abbeville P, 1980.

_____. *Zane Grey: Outdoorsman.* Englewood Cliffs, NJ: Prentice-Hall, 1972.

_____. *Profiles in Saltwater Angling*. Englewood Cliffs, NJ: Prentice-Hall, 1973.

Reiger, John F. *American Sportsmen and the Origins of Conservation*. Winchester P, 1975.

Reisner, Marc. *Game Wars: The Undercover Pursuit of Wildlife Poachers*. New York: Penguin, 1991.

Rooney, John F., and Richard Pillsbury. *Atlas of American Sports*. New York: MacMillan, 1992.

Rossi, Peter H. "The Presidential Address: The Challenge and Opportunities of Applied Social Research." *American Sociological Review* 45.6 (1980).

Roth, Richard P. "The Adirondack Guide (1820-1919): Hewing Out an American Occupation." Diss. Syracuse U, UMI, 1990.

Rundell, P. "Angling in Ancient Times." *Sports Afield* Nov. 1984.

Safari Club International Conservation Fund. "Profile: The Issue is Hunting." Tucson: n.d.

Salten, Felix. *Bambi*. New York: Grosset and Dunlap, 1929.

Schmitt, Raymond L., and Wilbert M. Lenoard, II. "Immortalizing the Self Through Sport." *American Journal of Sociology* 5 (Mar. 1986).

Schultz, K. "Is There a Giant Fish in Your Future?" *Field and Stream* 90.8 (1985).

Self, Margaret Cabell. *The Hunter: In Pictures*. Philadelphia: Macrae Smith, 1972.

Shaw, Dale. "The Hunting Controversy: Attitudes and Arguments." Diss. Colorado State U, 1973.

Shaw, William Wesley. "Sociological and Psychological Determinants of Attitudes Toward Hunting." Diss. U of Michigan, 1974.

Singer, Peter. *Animal Liberation: A New Ethics for Our Treatment of Animals*. New York Review Book. Random House, 1975.

_____. *The Expanding Circle: Ethics and Sociobiology*. New York: Farrar, Straus & Giroux, 1981.

Sofranko, Andrew, and Michael F. Nolan. "Early Life Experiences and Adult Sports Participation." *Journal of Leisure Research* 4.1 (1972).

Sosin, M., ed. *Angler's Bible*. South Hackensack, NJ: Stoeger Pub., 1975.

Spinrad, William. "The Function of Spectator Sports."*Handbook of Social Science of Sport*. Eds. Gunther R.F. Luschen, and George H. Sage. Champaign, IL: Stipes, 1981.

Standish, Burt. *Frank Meriwell's Hunting Trip*. Philadelphia: David McKay, 1903.

Starr, D. "Equal Rights." *Audubon* Nov. 1984.

Stone, G.P. "American Sports: Play and Display." *Mass Leisure.* Eds. E. Larrabee and R. Meyersohn. Glencoe, IL: Free, 1958.

Thomas, Richard H. *The Politics of Hunting.* Aldershot, England: Gower Pub. Co., Ltd, 1983.

Thurnau-Nichol, C. "Hook, Line and Sinker: Taking the Bait of the Fishing Industry through Hyping the Great Outdoors." Paper presented at the Midwest Sociological Society meetings, St. Louis, MO, 1985.

*Time.* 8 Sept. 1986: EB6.

*Times-Courier.* Associated Press, Charleston, IL. 31 Mar. 1986: B12.

_____. 25 Sept 1992: Cl.

Toffler, A. *Future Shock.* New York: Random House, 1970.

Tonso, William R. "Social Problems and Sagecraft: Gun Control as a Case in Point." *Firearms and Violence: Issues of Public Policy.* Ed. Don B. Kates. Pacific Institute for Public Policy Research, 1984.

Trefelthen, James B. *An American Crudade for Wildlife.* New York. Winchester P, 1975.

Trench, Charles Chenevix. *A History of Marksmanship.* Chicago: Follett, 1972.

Turner, E.S. All Heaven in a Rage. New York: St. Martin's, 1964.

U.S. Bureau of the Census. *Statistical Abstract of the U.S.:* 1987. 107th ed. Washington, D.C.

U.S. Bureau of the Census. *Statistical Abstract of the United States:* 1992. 112nd ed. Washington, D.C.: Superintendent of Documents.

U.S. Department of Commerce. *The Statistical History of the United States from Colonial Times to the Present.* Washington, D.C.: Bureau of the Census, 1960.

U.S. Department of Commerce. *Statistical Abstracts of the United States.* Washington, D.C.: Bureau of the Census, 1981-83.

Vitali, Theodore. "Sport Hunting: Moral or Immoral?" *Environmental Ethics* 12 (Spring 1990).

Waterman, Charles F. *A History of Angling.* Tulsa: Winchester P, 1981.

_____. *The Part I Remember.* New York. Winchester P, 1974.

_____. *The Treasury of Sporting Guns.* New York: Random House, 1979.

*Webster's New Collegiate Dictionary.* Springfield, MA: G. & C. Merriam Co., 1975.

*Webster's New Twentieth Century Dictionary.* William Collins Publishers, Inc., 1979.

Weidner, Ruth Irvin. "Images of the Hunt in Nineteenth Century America and Their Sources in British and European Art." Diss. U of Delaware. UMI, 1988.

Weiss, J. "The Confusing Issue of Catch and Release." *Bass Master Magazine* Jan 1981.

Whisker, James B. *The Right to Hunt.* North River P, 1981.

Whitney, Elliot (H.L. Sayler). *The Giant Moose.* Chicago: Reilly & Britton, 1912, 1936.

_____. *Mankiller of the Foothills.* Chicago: Reilly & Lee, 1912, 1936.

Wilkinson, Frederick, ed. "The Evolution of the Gun." *The Book of Shooting for Sport and Skill.* New York: Crown, 1980.

Williams, T. "Fishing to Win." *Audubon* May 1984.

_____. "Hiking the Tournament Trail." *Gray's Sporting Journal* 10.4 (Spring 1985).

Wilson, Edward O. *On Human Nature.* Cambridge, MA: Harvard U, 1978.

Wooldridge, John. "High Tech Help." *Chevy Outdoors.* Lintas Marketing Communications Apr./May 1993.

Yarnell, Duane. *Through Forest and Stream.* Cleveland: World Publishing, 1949.

Zgonina, Tim. "National Hunting and Fishing Day." *Times-Courier* Charleston, IL. 25 Sept. 1992: Cl.

# SUBJECT INDEX

**175**

# NAME INDEX